ONE
WHITE
STONE
JOURNEY
OF FAITH

daniel posney

ONE WHITE STONE

ISBN:0990527603
ISBN-13:9780990527602

DEDICATION

This book is dedicated to you. Thank you for causing *One White Stone* to become manifested.

ONE WHITE STONE

CONTENTS

Acknowledgments — i

1 Introduction — Pg 1

2 Our Journey Begins — Pg 3

3 The Gift — Pg 15

4 Right Relationship — Pg 21

5 Addictions And Attachments — Pg 32

6 Expectation Is The Cause Of Suffering — Pg 33

7 Letting Go Of The River Bank — Pg 43

8 Own Your Words and Speak The Poetry Of Love — Pg 52

9 You Are Worthy And You Are Loved — Pg 58

10 Fear And Death — Pg 64

11 You Are Not Obligated — Pg 72

12 Making Love With Life — Pg 76

13 It's All About Intention — Pg 85

14 We Are Divine Beings — Pg 88

15 The Big Questions — Pg 93

16 Living In The Heart As A Creator — Pg 105

17 You Are Dreaming — Pg 118

ONE WHITE STONE

18   Ecstasy And Bliss   Pg 120

19   Our Deepest Longing   Pg 124

20   The Inevitable Reality   Pg 126

ACKNOWLEDGMENTS

Cara Marie Petrone
Shirley & Hank Carey
Jim Michaelson
Jeannine Michaelson
Helen King
Crystal Starweaver
John & Prema Lia Thompson
Charles Jacquin
Shara Summers & Dale Pathe
Ascension Earth Network
Martin Ball, Phd.

Angels who helped fund my journey:
Jim Michaelson
(Blue Island World)
Greg Collison
(LosAlamosRealEstateCompany.com)
Anahata Chakra
(ShamangelicHealing.com)
Mike Shuler
(theShulerGroupInc.com)

ONE WHITE STONE

INTRODUCTION

It's a funny thing writing a book. I started writing while sitting in a 200sq ft. cabin on 4000 acres of rural land, within a spiritual community. As we all do in different ways, the writings were "channeled" and flowed as inspired words (as opposed to thought). As I ingested these concepts from higher consciousness, the pathways in my brain were created and reformed. My heart continued to feel more expansive and alive. I experienced feeling more empowered and liberated from the inherent pains normally associated with physical life. Over time, I started to organize the content and put it all into a form. Even as did this and acknowledged living life from this new understanding, more realizations, concepts, perceptions and epiphany had to be added. So, I added…and it grew. As the words became my life, I accepted more of myself and became more of what I knew was there, waiting. Eventually, I realized that we are all saints and bodhisattvas waiting to fully accept and love ourselves. This idea (that we are saints and *bodhisattvas-in-waiting*) caused me a good deal of discomfort, because I had left those ideas to legend, myth and others worthy of such distinctions.

This is a true story of divine awakening, spiritual experience, of learning and practicing conscious communication and cultivating love relationships more expansive than ever thought possible. This book will empower you, if you let it.

One White Stone is waiting to serve as a guide for creating a more perfect and healthy body, of easing and eliminating suffering, for transforming your life and those of others into your greatest joy and fulfillment. It has assisted me to realize my own self worth and to completely love myself, to overcome fear and death, learn how to serve humanity, change the world, "make love" with life and to become the master of my Self. *One White Stone* assists with the questions "Who Am I?", "What Am I?" and "Why Am I Here?".

Lightworkers, Visionaries, Wayshowers, Mystics, Creative Geniuses, Boat-Rockers, Button-Pushers, Trouble-Makers, Whistle-Blowers and Saints, Masters Of Flow and Bodhisattvas, thank you for attracting this book. I feel you will most resonate with this story and the timeless wisdom that has been channeled here. My wish is that the consciousness in the words of this book will guide you towards living ever more in your heart as a creator, as well as knowing, accepting and allowing your deepest longing. This is your inevitable reality.

One White Stone isn't for everyone, but it is for *you*. Somewhere close or deep inside you, you are already aware of the concepts and perspectives which are presented in these pages. I love you.

OUR JOURNEY BEGINS

Now, the story of the white stone begins with
my twin brother and I, in the Pacific Ocean, at
the end of a hot, summer day of body-surfing
Zuma Beach in California. The dry, hot, beach
sand was scorching on our feet, so we were
enjoying the cool water and beautiful waves.
"One more wave!" I joyfully, yelled to Ken.
Wow, famous last words. There was a tiny voice
inside of my head trying to get my attention. At
this part of my life, I hadn't started to listen to
this small voice, and now it was trying to tell me
that the late-in-the-day waves were getting
more "hollow", as if the face of the rising waves
were being carved out. At the same time, the
ever-changing tide was going back out to sea,
making the bottom of the wave shallow and
creating an ominous and dangerous landing
zone.

Ken and I were now in our 40's and we had
been body-surfing since we were kids, growing
up in California. We used to make the 25-mile,
round-trip journey, with our friends, from Garden
Grove all the way to the beach. If we had been
mowing lawns for the neighborhood (towing
the lawnmower behind our bikes) and we

4

hadn't spent the money on pinball games, beef jerky and candy, we'd take the city bus. Otherwise, we'd ride our BMX bikes, popping wheelies and doing "kick-outs" (causing our rear wheel to jump up and over to one side) onto each other's bikes. Either way, by bus or bicycle, it was a long trip by the time we got home. All day at the beach and we'd be blissfully, fried to a crisp and happy to be home to Fritos and tuna sandwiches and a sugary dose of Kool-Aid (just add one bucket of white sugar to a tablespoon of flavor packet) or "*How about a Nice Hawaiian Punch!?*" Our parents never kept us from experiencing the fullness of life and they encouraged it. By the time we were twelve, we'd travel to England, Scotland, Austria, Denmark and then several weeks in Africa. My father had worked two mechanical engineering jobs, for years, to afford the trip. Glenn died in an early-morning car crash before the epic trip and there was my super-courageous Mom with three kids (two, twelve-year old twin sons and a fourteen-year old daughter), in Africa. That must have been extremely trying on the nerves and emotions. Thankfully, us boys were perfect angels and just tried to do our best to keep our sister behaved. At fifteen years old, Ken and I took scuba-diving lessons and would each rent a sleek, fourteen-foot catamaran in San Diego's Mission Bay.

One last wave.

As I caught that looming wave, I felt the unstoppable surge of the ocean change the wave's form into something scary and there was no escape out of it. I could feel my 150lb. body lifted up and, as gravity took over, I saw the sand below. The wave, which seemed to have turned into a giant hand, made of water, grabbed my body and slammed it down with authority.

I had been in "mermaid" position, so my hands where behind me when I landed, forehead first, into the sand. There was definitely a "craaack" heard in the water as my back responded to the jolt.

Ken was there to meet me as I cautiously and gingerly stumbled out of the ocean. "Are you ok?" he asked. "I don't think so." were all the words I could put together. A minor concussion was the answer from my family doctor. Later, I was watching a surfing documentary that told a story of a young, up-and-coming, professional surfer who had almost the same experience and had become partially paralyzed. It was haunting. You know, as I look back at all of the crashes, spills, blood, flips, trips, scuba diving, surfing, sailing, fast driving, "irresponsible" behavior and over 100,000 miles of motorcycle riding...I'm just not meant to die yet! As a kid, I often wondered what was going to be my "mark". You know, was I going to be famous as an inventor, or in a successful band, or act? I didn't know, but I felt that somehow, I was different. Not better or special, just different.

I didn't slow down after the body-surfing accident. On the outside, I had a minor concussion, interior bleeding caused my skin to turn blood red, but no permanent damage..*that I that I that I know of*. On the inside, something was shifting. I still had the occasional floating episodes, while lying in bed. Then, there was the vibrating hum that I heard and felt. It sounded like a spaceship coming in to land. It permeated throughout my entire body, to the core. At times, it was somewhat uncomfortable because of the areas that I felt probed, but I promised myself I would start to allow the feeling and explore what it all meant. I finally did fully understand these episodes, after a particularly, intense lucid dream. I felt myself awake, probed and being brought up to a ship. Inside, on a gurney, I was wheeled around a metallic, semi-circular passageway.

Other people were being led back to Earth. It felt like a check-up.

"SQWOCK! SQWOCK!" one day, I opened my sleepy, early-morning eyes to see a three-foot tall, excited raven, wings spread, jumping up and down, angrily, on my bed and squawking at me incessantly. "My eyes are open. I'm awake" I said to myself. I blinked my eyes and moved my eyes around the room. Yes, it was my room and I was awake.
"There..is..a..big..black..bird on my bed". In the coming weeks and months, I soaked up everything I could related to spiritual awakening, energy, psychic abilities, astral travel and dreaming. I also started to develop an "ecstatic breathing" class, similar to "holotropic" breathwork or "re-breathing" (used by psychiatrist Stanislav Grof and others) where I would promote deep, fast, rhythmic breathing and combine it with evocative music and instrumentals (didgeridoo, Native American flute, drum...etc.). This was the start of my spiritual awakening. It was coming in fast. I was happily becoming the part of my family that was "new-agey" and a bit kooky. My emotions became increasingly strong and the beauty of life, music and who I was becoming was almost too much to take. I remember after seeing a

8

moving and inspiring performance from Hawaiian slack-key guitarist and singer George Kahumoku, I called my brother. "Sometimes the beauty is too much" I told him, sobbing afterwards. For me though, it wasn't something that could be turned off. It wasn't a phase and it wasn't sadness or depression. It was joy and bliss. Once you start to wake up, there's just no going back to being asleep. That's not to say there weren't times that I desperately wanted to get off that train! Life seemed to be less work and less complicated after a couple of gin-and-tonics instead of remembering the spectacular truth of who I really am.

Even being in a second marriage to a multi-millionaire, with five homes in exclusive Santa Barbara, I couldn't fall in line. You would think that I could just put everything aside or in the closet, while I enjoyed the good life. But, that's not me. Looking back now, I created that as a validation or sort of right-of-passage. Kind of a "what are you willing to give up to be in your truth?" experience. During that relationship there was lots of alcohol and not talking about the "elephant in the room". Sexual intimacy was full of problems. My cholesterol was in the high 200's and I was competing in triathlons and training for my black belt in hapkido. After the relationship came to an abrupt end, my path got back on track, I quit drinking and eating meat and cut my sugar intake way down. Without all the stress and poor diet, within weeks my cholesterol was restored to around 160.

Relationships had changed, challenged and totally sky-rocketed my understanding of communication and what a relationship was all about. I remember clearly the day Debbie calmly told me "If you're upset with something I say, it's your stuff. I'm just a mirror of that trait within you. It's called a 'trigger'. Any negative trait you have will be amplified just so it will be loud and clear and it will continue to be brought up in your life for you to work with and heal until it is completely healed to your satisfaction. You will want to own your triggers in order to find out where they come from. It's like a cup of water with sediment (our trauma) at the bottom. We live life through that sediment. But, stir it up and it moves towards the surface, to be looked at and cleared."

Holy what-the-hell! But I...you can't...it's not me...you. Um, yeah. Slowly, but inevitably, I would understand, but it took a while. I found out that even the Toltecs say "Everyone is a reflection - the reflection is something you have judged about yourself. It may have been exiled. It may not."

When you are "triggered", be calm and learn to hold the feeling or emotion and experience it but, don't react with it. It was your past reaction that was causing the upset. You were triggered and were reacting due to a history that you had. Find out where the reaction comes from. Looking at it will lessen its power over you. Needless to say, this four-year relationship transformed me. It was during this time that I became a mentor in the Munay-Ki (Love Energy), a healer's journey onto a path of selflessly, serving humanity. Munay-Ki is a set of nine, sacred and ceremonial rites that tend to uncover hidden traumas or blockages and challenge you to fully heal them. It is only going through this type of uncovering that we can truly help others heal. In fact, when we heal ourselves, we heal others and not only others, but the energy of that issue on all levels and on all dimensions.

It was during the practice of these nine rites that I came face-to-face with a decision to ask myself where I stood in my own truth. Many people, at around the 3rd rite, will back out due to relationship disputes that can arise or because of the lack of desire to go that deep into one's emotions and trauma. I forged through and came out the other side transformed and feeling fully empowered.

The spiritual path can be a series of milestones of inner truth and declaration of your greatest desires. It seems that people are put in front of us, silently asking us "How strong are you on this? How dedicated are you to your inner transformation and that of raising the vibration of the planet and the collective consciousness of humanity?". It may look like these people are standing in our way, but no one stands in our way. This is only the physical perspective in the purely "3D" reality. On the soul level or what some name the "5D" (and beyond), we are divinely-guided and fully supported by everyone and everything. We are "tuned" to our own perspective. If you want to experience your God-like nature as a whole and divine being, then seek to experience another perspective found through others. Change your perspective and you change your life.

In the sci-fi movie *The Matrix*, the movie's hero, Neo, is offered one of two pills to swallow. The red pill will take him "down the rabbit hole" and show him the truth and reality of his existence, as difficult as that may be to "swallow". The blue pill will allow him to stay believing his current reality and blissfully ignorant. Of course, there would be no movie if he didn't take the red pill, which he does. This leads to the understanding that he has been a slave to a system of greed, fear and corruption. It's a difficult awakening to have. It helps me to understand, as best that I can, that not everyone wants to know another possibility. It's not important that they do, only that I do. Hmm, did I take the red pill or the blue pill?

The "collective consciousness" (the blue pill) is the default awareness and is a measurable, energetic field on our planet. Scientists have tracked this field and found that when important events were about to happen, the measurements would change in a specific way. So, by watching these measurements, they can start to actually predict important events. This "collective" is what your reality is without doing any waking up or trying to seek your own truth. It's this "vibration of the masses" that allows violence to be accepted and wars to be fought. You can be part of the collective consciousness, the default, or raise your own consciousness. Ask yourself "How much and what kind of violence is acceptable?" If violence is acceptable in your life, then it is acceptable in your external reality.

Once you do start to wake up within this dream, the collective consciousness looks like insanity. This is one of the inherent pains of waking up, that of seeing the unsettling reality that you had been a part of and accepted without question for so long. Or maybe, you got the point (like most people) of seeing the reality and not accepting it and spending your day and night complaining about it You'd say how the government this, the President that, this country, that official. It's painful and emotionally draining and it gets easier, once you let go of all this struggle and fighting to stay in this reality. You start to notice that your life is beautiful and full of new wonder and amazement. You realize that the possibilities are actually limitless. Life transcends accepted society and your heart begins to open fully and completely.

Even this, this opening of the heart to everything, takes courage and I have found that for me, it was done as a conscious decision and one of allowing the emotion-flooded moments to flow fully through me. I had been told about the movie *Brother Sun, Sister Moon* from my family in the spiritual community in which I was a resident. The area that I lived on was a 4000-acre ranch, 40 miles north of Santa Barbara, California. The composer in the movie,

Donovan, provided the score for the film and was a friend of the community. Even though, everyone raved about the movie, I put it off for a while. I finally bought the film and brought it to the ranch's lodge to watch on their big screen TV. I hadn't owned a TV for over 8 years. So, the lodge was my huge living room, while I enjoyed renting an occasional movie. I was completely alone as I watched *Brother Sun, Sister Moon*. The beginning scenes of Francis of Assisi dancing amongst the posies made me think "I hope this gets better". I don't' know why I kept watching. But, I did. I guess I was determined that there was something there for me to see. There was one particular scene that tapped into the core of my being and ripped open my heart. After an awakening, Francis of Assisi is dragged, by his enraged father, to the local Bishop who asks Francis "Why do you act this way? What do you want?". Francis removes all of his clothes and gives them away and tells his father "I am not your son. You are not my father. I want to be as free as the birds in the air…" Heartbreaking, I'm sure, for the parents. But, I got it. I really understood this. You may have come to a point in your life, like I did, that your family knows who you are the least.

Later in the movie *Brother Sun, Sister Moon*,

against the warnings of his friends, Francis visits the Pope. He is abruptly turned away only to be called back by the Pope who seems to receive a divine inspiration. As Francis and his brethren are all accepted back into the lavishly-adorned chambers, the Pope slowly and intently makes his way down the royal steps to stand directly in front of the shabby monks. With the obvious contrast in religious life displayed in front of him and against the restraints of other clergy and with an awestruck look upon his face, the Pope bows down and lovingly kisses the tops of Francis' feet. I cried for over 45 minutes. I cried for the deep connection with Saint Francis' words and his desire to remove himself from "normal" village life and to totally serve God.

There are some that have found this service within a community, like the one I lived in, or within a particular religion. For me, I always felt there was something more beyond the dogma and limitations of holding onto a lineage. Being that the spiritual community, of which I was a part, mission was "self-realization", I couldn't help but ask myself "If self-realization is the mission, how could there be any judgment against any other consciousness-raising thought or method? How could one stay within a particular lineage if the goal is indeed self-

16

realization?". Our spiritual lineage, tools and practice (sadhana) can become an obstacle to further growth and realization. Legendary martial artist, Bruce Lee, spoke of and practiced *Jeet Kune Do,* which promoted "the way of no way" or "a boat to get one across and then discarded and not carried on one's back". Bruce taught to "flow like water", to have no fixed position. I like that.

THE GIFT

I had been "in service" (working for no charge) at a crystal store and healing center called *Aligning Light Center* in Sedona. When someone wasn't actively purchasing something from the shelves, I would sit quietly in one of the chairs around a circular table. Inevitably, a visitor would walk in "just browsing". Within minutes we were, most likely, connecting and they were moved to tears as their true feelings would come through. Sometimes it would turn into an hour-long counseling session and other times not. In every one, it was perfect. People would find it easy to open up to me and receive life-changing guidance with what was going on in their life. They would all leave empowered and enlightened with higher consciousness. I am honored to have shared space with Hopi elder, good witches, Cherokee medicine men and many other authentic lightworkers (people on a spiritual path) and other enlightened, awake human beings.

I started to have visitors who brought messages of a darker nature too. One day, a dark-complexioned man walked in. He looked like a drifter, like he'd been around the globe. He

18

wore a khaki shirt, blue jeans and a donut-shaped, black "pi" stone around his fifty-something-year-old neck. This stone is familiar to healers who are dedicated to the Nine Rites of the Munay Ki. This drifter walked straight up to me and said "I have a message for you". There's a lot of show going on in Sedona and this felt like something straight out of Indiana Jones. But, I chose to stay out of judgment, pay attention and listen to every word with quiet discernment. Besides, there were some synchronicities or coincidences that couldn't be ignored. He talked about being cautious of the dark forces, about the important role I was playing, the journey I was about to embark upon...and the return of Elvis. Hey, I'm open. I had very powerful dreams about the Amazon and Peru and this man was from the Amazon. During the lucid part of this dream about Peru and the Amazon, "Pumamayo" or "Lion of May" was planted into my brain. At the time, I didn't know exactly why it made me cry when I awoke from that dream. I ended up searching all over the internet for this elusive word ("Pumamayo") and I found that it's actually a small village in the mountains of Peru! This man introduced himself as "Paul" and, with his weathered and chocolate-colored skin and shiny, black hair, he talked about how he had lived in Santa Barbara, where I also lived for over thirteen years. His message was a warning and a validation. He was one of several visitors I recently had who were speaking about the more darker aspects of spirituality.

This kind of thing, the strange and synchronistic connections, seemed to be happening more and more over those few months. While sitting with Cara in my favorite coffee shop (*Bad Kitty Koffee*), another man named Michael, who had been sitting near us, said "I have something to give you". In Sedona, people are always giving each other crystals and exotic stones, which are promised to have special powers and such. In fact, I had an intense experience with a 5ft long crystal causing me to be physically repulsed and uneasy when approaching it. It wasn't until spending more time acclimatizing myself with the surrounding crystals that I could approach and touch this huge crystal. People were always asking me if I "felt anything with this one". It was actually rare that I felt something from a Lemurian crystal or Arcturian something or other. From his small, leather, medicine pouch, Michael pulled out a simple, white stone.

I vaguely recalled the ancient stories of the use of white stones. For the Polynesian ancestors, in their times of conflict, a white stone and a black stone were taken to the chief of a neighboring island tribe. As the legend goes, if the sometimes unfortunate messenger presented the stones and a black stone was taken by the chief, this meant war between the two tribes. Otherwise, if the white stone was chosen, peace would prevail. As Roman gladiators would prepare for deadly games, they were allowed to blindly pick a stone from a bucket of stones. If a white stone was picked, he received the day off and would not have to fight that day. Even the Bible (Revelations) includes a passage which speaks of receiving a white stone: *"And he who has an ear, let him hear what The Spirit speaks to the assemblies: 'To the one who is victorious I shall give of the manna which is hidden, and I shall give him a white pebble, and upon the pebble, a name in writing that no man knows except he who receives."*

"You need to bring this stone to the waters of Mount Shasta", Michael said. I felt my mouth drop and I couldn't hide my amazement. In California? Why did I keep hearing about Mount Shasta? I knew the answer to my own question. How far down the proverbial "rabbit hole" do you want to go, Daniel? I felt my world starting to spin. I continued to open myself up to new and exciting adventures and possibilities.

Mount Shasta, California. Mount Shasta is said to be more of a spiritual home for a lot of people. Legends abound and many spiritual seekers find their way to the incredible beauty of that mountain and its community. I continued to hear about Mount Shasta from people who had visited the sacred mountain and others who were also planning trips there. Many people consider Sedona, Arizona, a very spiritual place. Sedona might be better described as a place with very, strong energy and lots of opportunity for inner transformation. The vortexes, ancient ruins and natural rock formations. They all attract seekers of spiritual transformation and it does happen there, for sure. Local Native Americans journeyed to Sedona for spiritual cleansing and vision quest...but, didn't live there. Now, there's all sorts of classes and workshops, retreats, activations and channeling with "non-physical beings". It seems like everyone is a Reiki Master and licensed massage therapist. Sedona does have many authentic healers and guides and this was mostly my experience. Though, I did run across a few actors and acts, it's all part of the collection of residents and wanderers. Your inner voice gets very clear and it does become easier to discern who has broken their self down and retired their spiritual ego and who hasn't. "Spiritual ego" is when we get caught up in our own spiritual path and feel the need to continually vomit it out to others at every opportunity "I'm more enlightened than you". They've lost the ability to be students. It seems to be a natural part of the process. You're so excited about sharing this new information and you want everyone to wake up too.

Sitting in a coffee shop, in Sedona, I was listening to music on my headphones. There were a lot of young people gathering for the transition from the casual, daytime coffee shop into a lively bar scene. There was a song playing in my headphones by chant artist *Snatam Kaur*, called *"Ong Namo"*. She sings about "coming home" and I heard it as "come home to God – to your true, divine nature". Like spiritual guru Ram Dass states *"We're all just walking each other home."* In that moment, I felt the outstretched hand of God calling me home. I knew I couldn't push this away any longer.

RIGHT RELATIONSHIP

It took me time to realize that when my partner and I were in an argument, due to my trigger, that I needed to stop thinking and stop letting my brain take over and instead let my heart take over. It knows what to do. The ego just wants to validate its existence. Any time you start to think about what to do, that's the wrong place to start...what does your heart say? It's the most difficult thing to reverse your course in mid-stream and say "I am wrong", but my partner could do it. It would leave me grasping. My ego didn't know what to do with that. So, I'd think of something that was sure to piss her off. She'd lovingly and peacefully hold her ground. She shared with me another term. It's called "holding space". It's an agreement to do your best to project only loving thoughts to the triggered person, as they experience being affected by your actions. We all have our own triggers and appreciate how helpful it can be for someone to be in a loving energy of allowing and not be triggered by another trigger. This is "holding space". By me not feeding the fire, we can resolve any anger and evolve into a higher consciousness. During these conflicts, the person holding space can ask "And what else?" and wait and ask again until the other person has been entirely heard. If this process is not done and the issues are not addressed, this episode will surely play itself out again. This changed my life and my relationships. All of them. Whether intimate or family and friends. You don't need to push against anything or to convince anyone of anything. The person that you think is pushing against you is actually giving you the greatest gift, the gift of your own self-realization.

I agree with Neale Donald Walsh (author of *Conversations With God*), that at some level of consciousness the purpose of our relationships is to create an opportunity for growth, for full self-expression, for lifting our lives to their highest potential, for healing every false thought or small idea we ever had about ourselves, and for ultimate reunion with God through the communion of our souls. Ok, so this wasn't always the case as some of my past relationships may attest. But, hopefully, we all grow up and wake up.

EXERCISE: Take a moment with me now and feel that gratitude for each and every love relationship that you've ever had...mmm. See the gift in each one. I do. Yes, even that one.

Now, feel the peace in knowing the gift that you and I also gave to the other person. Know that, in the same way, you and I were a gift of unfathomable benefit. You and I deserve every bit of love, gratitude and thankfulness for giving what we knew how to give, in the way that was a match for what the other person was attracting.

Several "wayshowers" have taught me about the dynamics of emotions and reactions. Like, "Nobody can make you feel anything". No one can make you happy, you do that. In those moments, we all have a choice. Thoughts come before emotions. People are just playing the roles in our lives that we have asked them to play. Everyone is another aspect of yourself experiencing life in another way, a way which that individualized soul chose to experience.

Wayshowers and teachers told me to eliminate criticism and sarcasm. To begin with, practice no sarcasm and only honest, uplifting words for three days. Flirting and playfulness is fun and gets the creative juices flowing. Teasing, poking fun and sarcasm are manipulation and control tactics and are a screen to your true feelings. Refrain from sexual innuendo that dominate and puts each other down. Set agreements for your own responsibilities and your intentions for this relationship. Bring up any issues in the moment without reaction. If possible, do not wait for a more appropriate moment. Use "I" statements. No blame game. Both of you get to ask for what you want. When there is a suggestion about an idea, express three things that you like about the idea, express a concern (if you have one) and then make a suggestion. Remember to: Praise. Critique. Praise.

While I was in Sedona, there was this build up of huge life change and spiritual devotion. I could feel my body out of alignment with what I knew was trying to happen. I wanted to have an unwavering focus on my love of God and a commitment to be of service. I started to get a feel for what others must experience when confronted with this ripping open of the heart and longing of the soul. I could feel the frustration with myself and wanted to continue hiding and not give up the amazing relationship and friendship Cara and I cultivated. Because of the previous inner work that we had both separately done before we met, our intimacy had reached high levels of divine expression and connection. The love that we were able to express and share with others had deep impacts on the people around us. I had developed a close bond with her two children.

Cara had her own epiphanies and would say "Every breath can be a gift and a rebirth. With every inhale you take, receive the gift from Spirit and with every exhale, offer it to Spirit." We were both in tears together over the coming loss. We agreed that an amazing, beautiful, fun, fulfilling, honoring, intimate relationship can be a beautiful sidetrack from our own separate divine path. Over the years, I had been informed, by different sources, that a relationship in this time of huge spiritual growth wouldn't really be the best thing...it didn't say "don't", just "not the best". I guess I wanted to prove that I still had free will and the fact is that I love relationship. I'm glad I did "buck the system" a bit. Every one of my relationships have been critical to my path and full of love and healing. So, Cara and I decided to see the perfection of the next phase of our lives. There's a crucial time during a "completion of a phase of a relationship" which we've been taught leads to argument and closing down. It's just "the way it is". Not so. This paradigm is broken. We have moved to another phase, which includes love, respect, compassion and grace.

If you find that you have come to the end of your relationship, honor this time. You can do this by seeking to understand what part of the relationship is not in the natural path of your joy. This is not a time for blame. Conditions change. People change. Desires change. You may have completed your "spiritual contract" with each other and staying in the relationship will delay further progress on your particular life path. If there are feelings of "you did this to me", realize your own part in this situation. Do not beat yourself up over it and place more guilt on yourself. Understand the dynamics and heal it to the best of your ability. If you blame others and don't take ownership for your creation and the very powerful manifestation of the situation, you will continue to see it in other subsequent relationships. Consciously transition from this relationship to a period of deep reflection and inner discovery. A "Disconnection Ceremony" can assist in honoring your partner and to show gratitude for the gifts you both received during the relationship. This ceremony, which celebrates the love that you have shared, is also used to "cut the cords" with grace and allow something greater to come into both of your lives.

While accepting and living this type of life path, there were many times that I asked myself "Why should I create more work for myself, if life is tough enough as it is? Why don't I just buck-up and live life like I did in the past and like millions of others do?" First of all, I remembered how really unhappy and disempowered I felt. The good news is that, when you do choose a path of awakening, you won't be experiencing the same burden or living the same life that you did before. You will start to master your life.

What about people who aren't on a spiritual path or even one that includes self-improvement? They might be filled with deep resentment, anger and angst. How do we deal with them if we don't normally attract them in our daily lives, but are there when we visit our relatives or attend reunions? Here's a story that I hope helps to explain working with this scenario.

After flagging down a New York City taxi cab, a woman asked to be taken to Grand Central Station. They were driving in the right-hand lane when, all of a sudden, another car pulled out of a parking space right in front of them. The taxi driver slammed on his brakes, skidded, and missed the other car's back end by inches! The driver of the other car, the guy who almost caused a big accident, whipped his head around and started yelling at the taxi driver. The taxi driver just smiled and waved at the guy in a friendly way. The taxi passenger was still shocked and upset so, she asked, "Why did you just do that? This guy almost ruined your car and sent us both to the hospital!" The taxi driver told her "The Law of the Garbage Truck." Many people are like garbage trucks. They run around full of garbage, full of frustration, full of anger, and full of disappointment. As their garbage piles up, they need a place to dump it. And if you let them, they'll dump it on you. When someone wants to dump on you, don't take it personally. You just smile, wave, wish them well, and move on. There is only one thing that these people desire. Love. Unconditional love.

Some people like to use the term "anger issues". Anger is a temporary, natural emotion when you have not accepted what IS. Anger can be a motivator towards a course of action. Anger can move you from depression. The man, angry at the taxi driver, hopefully got the anger flushed out of his system. We rarely are aware of what is going on in a stranger's life. Sometimes, we connect with them just so the emotions can be released. Even an attacker is calling out for help and for love that he or she does not feel he or she deserves. Love the bully and he will transform.

Masters are not ruled or governed by their emotions. As humans, we tend to have two different ways of living with emotions. One way is as a victim of the emotion, allowing it to rule your life and be the cause of great upset. The other way is to push the emotions or traumas down into the depths of your being, usually becoming lodged within your physical body as energy and manifesting as disease, illness and abnormal growths and rashes. When we choose to heal, we are healing lifetimes of trauma. When it comes to healing the body, there is only actually healing in the mind and really not *healing*, but *aligning* with truth. As the mind is not limited to just being local, all healing covers all time and space. Admit or be open to further healing. Ninety-nine percent of past trauma may be healed, or aligned. Accept the possibility that one percent may still need to be healed. This does not mean that you have to then start at the beginning.

It is okay to express our emotions. But, remember to be constructive and not get lost in the drama of your emotions. If you find yourself stuck in your emotions, you can say "It is my will that I allow this emotion to express and be released in a healthy and effective way." We are emotional beings. We emit vibrations related to our emotions when we have emotional episodes or outbursts. This is why after a couple has had an argument, the unsettling feeling in the room can be felt long after they are gone.

During a trip to Utah with a group of psychics and lightworkers, My partner and I had occasion to rent a hotel room. We walked in the room and it felt like a government interrogation office, like all of the life had been sucked out of it. It felt dead. I down-played it with my partner, but the more I tried the more irritated I became with her. She wanted to "sage" the room (wafting burning white sage smoke while performing a short ceremony) and I just became even more upset, not believing in this airy-fairy stuff. Finally, the Lakota-descendant leader of our group walked in, smiled and validated that were was definitely something off about the room. They lit a white sage bundle and I could physically tell that the room shifted and it felt as if it was re-infused with life energy. The next day, as we prepared to leave, we asked the hotel managers about the history of that room which was next to their office. They admitted that a teen, runaway girl had been staying in the room and later been murdered. I learned a huge lesson that day.

If you are upset by someone, you have the choice to start to look at your own involvement in the situation. Why is it that this person caused you to be upset? Would anyone else have become upset? Why did you create this episode? Before we accuse others, first ask of yourself "Could I accuse myself of this?" Here's the dichotomy: things aren't happening to you. They are just happening. It is your reaction to what is happening that is creating your reality and your suffering. When they are happening, you are involved in it because you have attracted it to yourself.

If you are feeling negative emotion, you are "paddling upstream". Quit paddling upstream. I know what it feels like to just want to be upset. In that moment, if someone had asked me "Do you want to stay upset?". I might have said "Yes, right now, I want to be upset!" If you don't want to stay upset, then let your boat change direction and float downstream towards the natural joy of life. One of the ways that you can get out of the upset is to take a breather and be with your thoughts. Sometimes this works for me when I can honestly listen to the thoughts and see that they don't really make sense and usually are coming from a damaged ego. If you find yourself in a slump, I have found it helpful to connect with people and serve them.

Remember, you are the creator of your life and you will cause yourself to bring in episodes of life that are for your highest good and greatest evolution towards Oneness and release of the illusion of separation between You and All That Is. If you are unhappy, ask yourself what is the cause of the unhappiness. Remember, which came first…the emotion or the thought? Didn't a thought trigger the emotion?

EXERCISE: Find something to laugh about. You could laugh at the absurdity of trying to find something to laugh about. Do this in public. See what happens to people after they get over their speculation and judgments and join you in your laughter. You will transform their day!

EXERCISE: Breathing & Smiling. While you are experiencing negative emotions, breathe deeply while counting slowly to 5, then count back down during your exhale. After 3 rounds, add a smile to your breathing. Now increase your smile. Notice the negative feelings cannot exist during this exercise.

ADDICTIONS & ATTACHMENTS

Most of us have addictions or attachments. Some of them are not healthy to our physical bodies. Having them can be a distraction, at the least. They are ways for us to distract ourselves from our divine nature, from the profound inner being that we find in the silence. Sometimes, these attachments are called "relationships" or "love". Spiritual teacher, OSHO, says that only those people who are capable of being alone are capable of love. He's not talking about a simple "I love you" towards another, but of sharing so deeply, without possessing the other, without attachment or addiction. Their happiness resides within themselves and not within another person. You could be capable of being alone, but only because you are too fearful of being with someone. So, there's more to it. Being capable of being alone and loving yourself. When you as happy alone as with someone, that is love. It's not the definition of love, though it is an example of what happens. When you are capable of loving yourself, this loves overflows and spills onto others.

If you find there is an attachment, use this as an

opportunity to uncover more of yourself. If this doesn't happen and you drop the attachment without the looking within, it will return stronger next time. This is like removing a cyst or taking pain medication. Find out why they are there, otherwise other warning signals (physical manifestations) will take their place. The next time you reach for an attachment, ask yourself what the cause may have been.

Attachments and addictions can be drugs and food or a type of relationship. But, they can also be yoga, meditation, seminars, workshops and seeking spiritual enlightenment. Attachments can be physical objects that carry certain memories. Letting go of objects that are no longer serving us really does much to clear the way, lighten the load and release the energy that is within those things. I have found that just spending a few moments with each item and honoring its place in my life, helped to fully release that item. This process also decreases your storage costs. One thing that helped me too was thinking that if anything happened to me, I wanted less for others to have to deal with, sort through and get rid of. The more that I let go of, the more room in my consciousness, more empty space and more peace. Mostly, we have attachment to outcome. We want things to turn out a certain way and will work very hard to try and make it happen. Going on a trip of faith really assisted me in realizing non-attachment to a specific outcome. I received so much more! Here's a list of what I experienced by releasing the attachment to control or plan the journey:

No motorcycle break-downs – Though the motorcycle was a beautiful, blue BMW, it was over 12 years old, with no normal/low-beam headlight (only high-beam), a critical oil leak and driven in all weather condition with a full load. It performed flawlessly.

No speeding tickets – During the trip, I normally travel between 75-90 mph.

Speaking Engagement – Helen completely organized an event ("Delicious Dialog, Heart Opening & Sound Healing") at Unity Church in Washington, which also allowed me to promote and pre-sell my book.

Gifts – I was gifted all manner of things, such as: orgon generator, crystals, books, greeting cards and a Native American flute.

Publisher/Editor contacts – I met publishers, John and Prema Lia Thompson from *Illuminated Arts* in Washington, who also became dear friends. John helped to heal a sore back that I was experiencing and Prema Lia gave me a spontaneous psychic reading that was right on. John also encouraged and guided me with ways to get *One White Stone* published and in front of publishers of very popular books of similar theme.

<u>Food & Lodging</u> – If there wasn't camping available, I always was provided a place to stay and food to eat. Sometimes, even laundry facilities and other amenities. Connection with friends and family became stronger and I always felt that it was mutually-beneficial.

EXPECTATION IS THE CAUSE
OF SUFFERING

If we didn't get caught up with our own
expectation, life would get easier. "I wanted to
get the lead role in the play!" or "I was hoping
for..." or "You should have..." or "I wish you
would have..." are all examples of
expectations that tend to cause us suffering.
When you can live without attachment to
outcome, you'll find your stress level goes way
down and your level of peace goes way up!

I found that expectation can also come in the
form of spiritual readings and channeling that
have a date associated with it. As humans living
a spiritual path, we can experience a flood of
"channeling" and readings from others
promising us great things, and having a date
attached to it can tend to be problematic.
When the promised date arrives with no
promised results, there's another story of why
the transformative event had to be delayed. It
can feel like the proverbial carrot in front of our
noses. There was always something to grab
onto. The truth is, it's not truth. It's not meant to
be truth. It's meant to be validation of your

beliefs. The first and second Universal Truths explain this. We create our reality and our life is a mirror. We bring this in to either validate or prefer. This is what propels creation. There are two ways of creating that you may be aware of. You are probably familiar with the idea of people perpetuating fear among the human race, through media, news of supposed terrorists attacks and advertisements of drugs that we need? Well, the other way is to perpetuate love among the human race. But, do not think that someone else is doing the perpetuating. We, as One being, are doing the perpetuating to create our own creation.

If you find yourself on a spiritual path, you will invariably come across psychics, readers, channels and Joe-the-plumber who have amazing abilities of working with non-physical beings and seeing energy. Many times, I have asked myself "Why am I not experiencing direct connection or experience as others seem to do? Am I not worthy of guidance on my spiritual path as others are?" Writing this book has been quite a journey. As I wrote these words, I found myself smack in the middle of a crushing, heart-breaking experience. I felt being continually lead on…that never-ending carrot in front of me. Of course, I've had thoughts like "What the heck am I doing? Should I just drop all this path and get a frickin' job? Maybe this whole thing about creating your reality is also an illusion." When I started to realize the attachment to spiritual path was falling away, I felt a twinge of fear. "But, what about this divine calling, the whole 'being of service' plan. If I don't feel like I belong anywhere? What if no one else sees what I see?" I tried to remember "A master stays out of the drama of the dream and observes" and to not focus on the clothes the teacher is wearing. Do not get lost in the scene or details. It took me to be fully immersed in the drama, until I began to question my reactions and my disappointment. What is truly important to me? What do I honestly require?

I realized that I had put a condition or effect on the way I truthfully and honestly chose to live my life. Living this way is the way that I'm going to live anyway, whether there's a pay-off or not. I choose to live my life from my heart and to love everything and everyone and to let go of everything that isn't love. And, there was something deep in there that was saying "If you live this way, there is great benefit to it" or "keep at it, because you will ascend to a higher dimension". This carrot always seemed to have some physical element to it. Prosperity.

Abundance. Physically living in a higher dimension. Meeting our extraterrestrial family. But, that's what keeps us going. In every part of our life, there seems to always be something to look forward to; sometimes "good" things and sometimes "bad". For some, it's a holiday, a war, a hug or touch, a meditation or the feeling of being here in this moment. These events keep our soul alive in the bodies that we exist within. Anticipation. Expectation. It's not the object, the goodies or the payoff that we desire in the end. it's the place that we are at and the way we feel at that moment that is the payoff.

EXERCISE: Try this for a day: live spontaneously. Live in the moment. Don't *plan* to shower or eat or meditate. Shower when you feel the need to shower. Eat when you are hungry. If you find yourself expecting, anticipating or thinking in the future, sit down or pull your car over (safely) and close your eyes for ten seconds. Get in touch with your breath and the feeling of it as it enters and exits your nostrils.

Since I haven't had a life of receiving divine messages, then "How do I devote myself to God, if I don't receive any messages of 'go here' or 'do this'?" I realized that I had forgotten one of the critical pieces of wisdom and that is to "be happy". If what you are doing isn't creating happiness, then stop doing it. This includes elements of a spiritual path. If this searching, finding "truth", discovering and awakening isn't causing happiness, question it. This is all a part of Self-Mastery. This has been huge for me. What? Let go of finding the truth? Stop waking up? If we only knew that we are already what we think we are trying to become, we could relax and enjoy the ride. We cannot strive to become something that we are not already. I have found that by letting go, I return to the truth of who I really am. Like peeling the skin from a ripe, juicy fruit. I uncover what was hidden and now is ready to be given as a delicious gift to whomever enjoys this type of fruit.

I am on the path that's best for me. I can see the default system that's currently available and I choose to create my own way. If your path includes becoming a master of your life, then you're telling yourself right now that you can complain about these hardships and disappointments, but eventually, you'll want to get back on the horse. We cannot not do it. It pulls at us with such determination and won't let go. We can try to delay it, but never stop it. We are all worthy of everything that we desire.

We are not given worthiness. There is no one granting worthiness to you, except yourself. We are inherently worthy of all of the joy, prosperity and love of the entire Universe, and more. For me, I still wanted to know "How do I deal with all of this stories and prophecies?" The answer that I received was this: What would you do if you were the "invisible coach" feeding you from the sidelines? Here you are, in a very challenging reality with promises and glimpses of another reality of almost inconceivable bliss and beauty. Humanity desires to get from this reality to another reality, to a higher consciousness. *Everyone* is assisting you towards this new reality, in *every* way. What would you feed You to keep You on track, motivated and creating? As another higher-consciousness version of yourself, if you knew the ultimate truth, where and how would you lead You? If one of the truths you wanted to experience and really understand was the truth that you are the Universe and there is nothing outside of you, how would you best get that across to you? If you really honestly thought about it, you would not cause yourself to become too dependent on outside sources (divine or otherwise) and guide yourself in a way that would still allow your own free will. But, what about others who do have experiences and communication with beings from other dimensions? Once again, I received an answer: Not everyone has the same path as you do. Again, there is no deciding that you don't get what others get. Everyone is being graced in the way that serves them for their highest good and their own soul's guidance. Our soul knows better than our ego knows. You may have wanted to really understand the awesome power that is inside of you...the truth of who and what you are. I realized that this was advanced stuff. If I could get this in this lifetime, I would have had physical experience of something that is a higher-dimensional concept. Now, to really give you a headache, contemplate the following theory, that every possible scenario is all happening at once, has happened and will probably happen again. No physical laws exist which would prohibit the existence of parallel worlds. So, in some other reality or dimension (which there are unlimited numbers), we are living the scenario that we're desiring.

It is never a lesson given to us for us to know suffering. We are the only one that has treated ourselves unfairly and we have been forgiven. All is well. Everything is in divine order. It is never that we must experience suffering in order to experience grace. Suffering is just expectation and not following your joy.

With suffering comes the feeling of being a victim or victimized. We are in victim consciousness if we think *anyone* can be a victim and does anything because of crimes perpetrated against them (i.e. a rapist has been sexually abused, someone is experiencing police brutality, an addict) or due to something "out of their control". When in victim consciousness, we give our power away. *Everyone* creates their own reality and our job is not to figure out or fix it. There are no victims.

Many people don't realize that when they choose to "fix" others that they may be interfering with their perfect path to their evolution and enlightenment. Their path of drugs and alcohol abuse may lead to them becoming a very inspirational and effective addictions counselor for thousands of other people suffering from addiction. Who are we to switch their train to our own "approved" track? Who are we to remove one of their stepping stones?

Am I saying to not address suffering in the world? No, I'm not. Here's the thing. Fix your own suffering within before trying to fix the suffering of others. We are not helpful if we do not do this first. If we receive joy by assisting to end the suffering of this world and our work is not being done because of guilt, then Yes, do what brings us joy. Still, in doing this, we are hoping to have more suffering in the world in order to bring us joy. Why not receive joy by ending our own suffering? Sometimes, we go way outside of ourselves to get away from our own self-inflicted suffering and this can be in the form of trying to save a third-world country or it may look like becoming a therapist.

There are no mistakes, only experiences. We are always giving the very best that we can with what we know, where we are and the level of consciousness that we exist within. All is love. Look at what was done "to you" and begin to challenge yourself to see it as Love. Do not look so closely at the physicality of it as much the divine purpose of it. Someone tries to oppress you. They demand things of you and cause great suffering in your life. Is this not a gift from someone who is also, like you, an aspect of All That Is? Could it be that this person's highest Self and You have agreed, on some level, to this episode of life experience. Can you see the pure love that it must have taken to provide for you an opportunity for forgiveness and the ability for you to take back your power and assert yourself?

Let go of outer stimulation and expectations. As you receive input from what seems like outer sources, allow and let them flow through or around you, whatever *you* choose. Don't be attached to them. Don't wait for the source to start flowing again, in anticipation. Go inside. Seek your own truth from your own source. Then, follow your bliss.

LETTING GO OF THE RIVER BANK

The great mystic, Joseph Campbell, says that we're in a freefall into the future and all you have to do to transform your hell into a paradise is to turn your fall into a voluntary act. Let go.

Looking at a swiftly-flowing river, notice how perfect everything is. Water flows gently around the obstacles. Imagine yourself hanging tightly onto a rock on the bank of the river. The struggle is intense and it literally wears you out. Let go of the riverbank. You are taken, by nature, directly to where the natural flow exists. Do you see how life "in the flow" is a dance?

Letting go allows us to receive so much. It's true that when you lovingly and consciously let go of material things, you make room for something better. Everything is taking up space in our mind. Create more space and allow the flow of Spirit and your joy to come through. There is prosperity, abundance, happiness and fulfillment when we let the natural flow of life in.

All this "letting go" and you might think I am what people like to call "commitment-phobic".

Actually, it's just the opposite. I love relationship. I am in relationship for the feeling of love that I have when I am with that person. We are in divine union, create love and make love in the tantric way. The tantric way is about tasting and experiencing all of life in a very full and complete way. All is sacred. All is beauty. Speech is poetry. Silence is ecstasy. Love is divine and precious. This all stems from loving myself first. When you love your own reflection then you can fully love someone else's. Let go of the past. Release yourself from the bondage of your thoughts. Forgiveness is key. Forgive unconditionally and completely.

One night, while sitting in the office at the spiritual sanctuary in California, I had a strong desire to call my twin brother. Ken answered "Howzit brah?" (Ken lives on the island of Kauai). I told him that I wanted to share a prayer of forgiveness with him. Ken was totally open to it and we said this prayer together.

"To all those that I have hurt knowingly or unknowingly, through thoughts, words, or actions…please forgive me." Take a deep breath and exhale the relief of this…

"To all those that have hurt me knowingly or unknowingly, through thoughts, words, or actions...I forgive you."

It was powerful. Ken said he had wanted to call me, as it had been eating away at him for a long time. He also apologized for an episode that he felt needed more forgiveness and it felt perfect. Later, I learned about "Ho' oponopono". Though people have had their own adaptations of "Ho'oponopono" (ho-o-pono-pono) which Wikipedia states "...is an ancient Hawaiian practice of reconciliation and forgiveness", I understand it as a way for us all to sit down and communicate to each other about what is going on in our lives and within our family. I find the following associated prayer very helpful with healing physical pains as well as emotional conflict.

"I am sorry.
Please forgive me.
I love you.
Thank you"

When he was finally released from a life-time of prison, Nelson Mandela said *"As I walked toward the gate that would lead to my freedom, I knew if I didn't leave my bitterness and hatred behind, I'd still be in prison."*

There has been much said about the rising of divine feminine and expressions of forgiveness from men to women. On the physical side of things, this is beautiful. There is also another step that is important. There is a further alignment to be initiated and that is associated with the brotherhood of men who are involved with the pursuit of their self-mastery.

As men have been associated with the conquering and domination of women, men can tend to feel lost in the pool of Divine Feminine Retreats and gatherings, which no attention given to men to also shift their awareness and claim their own divinity. For ultimate evolution and ascension, a *Brotherhood Of Self-Mastery* will be created, allowing men to stride in perfect step with the fully empowered and awakened woman. This is something that my friend and I have co-created. It takes a strong man to pursue fullness and to be vulnerable; he is not worried about losing anything, or showing himself as weak by expressing his feelings. Women can breathe deeply around self-assured men. There is a Cherokee proverb that goes something like this, *"A woman's highest calling is to lead a man to his soul, so as to unite him with Source. A man's highest calling is to protect woman so she is free* to walk the Earth unharmed." When you start to truly honor each other as the divine, instead of competing with them, your life changes in a powerful way. You are a force that is truly unbeatable. But, in order for this to be a possibility, we will want to get to a place of loving ourselves.

Forgiveness From Men To Men

To you my Brother, I apologize.

If I have ever done or said anything to hurt you, belittle you, offend you or emasculate you...please forgive me.

My knowledge of how to show love to my fellow man was limited, based in fear, and was not heart-centered. I did not know how to treat you as the Divine Being that you and I are.

Thinking this was how men loved other men, I used it as a way to pretend to raise myself up amongst our friends. I did not raise myself up. This was my insecurity as a man. I forgot that my challenges of being a man were the same challenges that you were experiencing.

No more. I have found
my own true strength.
You and I are connected
as One Being.

You are no less perfect
than any Sage, Master or Saint.
Brother, please receive this healing.

By acknowledging You and your natural
strength, intelligence, and protection,
I acknowledge and honor my own.

By offering guidance in Self-Mastery and
becoming a complete Being,
I will continue to teach myself.

With deep respect and love for you,
I will openly accept your wisdom
without judgment or competition.

Together in our brotherhood, may we both
become the complete Men that is our soul's
destiny, in this physical reality. And through
being an example of great men, we shall teach
other men to realize this and even more.

Together, we commit to teach
our sons these values and virtues.

ONE WHITE STONE

From Men to Women

If I, or any other man, have ever done anything to hurt you or offend you, and for the manifold transgressions against women, you and every other, I apologize.

Please forgive me and please forgive us.

If you have ever felt demeaned, un-cherished, or your womanhood betrayed in any way;

If I or any other man has failed to see the light of your sex and the brilliance of your female spirit, on behalf of all of us, I apologize.

May the beauty of women and the power of women and the vision of women now burst forth in our world and in our consciousness.

May the mind of man be healed. May the heart of woman repair. I commit to you and to God that I am, and shall be, a man who sees your value. I see your light.

God bless you and your sisters, our mothers and our daughters. I shall teach my sons to honor you.

Amen.

Surrender is another key to being fully awakened. Surrender is not about giving away power or anything of your Self. It is about preparing to receive all that is being offered you, that which you have been pushing away from. Surrender to the experience. Get into the natural flow of life. Let go of past deeds, fears, circumstances, revenge, mistakes and choose to forgive. Not letting go only causes suffering in you. Look around you and see how lives are sometimes lived driven by an ego. When you fight against forgiving, you are fighting against your own soul. Your ego is driving this fight to stay in drama and suffering. Can you see how you are causing only your own suffering? Every time you have a new thought against forgiving, you are proving that your ego is more powerful than You. It really isn't, but the ego part of you is doing its best to assert itself. It does this in a way that always tries to say "I'm only doing the best for you."

Michael Mirdad, Spiritual Director of Unity Church Of Sedona states "Know the truth, but respect the illusion". It is by fully embracing life that we experience grace. What is grace but divine influence, Oneness and connection with All That Is, while in the body, in this physical dimension.

Stop pushing against and having a fixed position. Letting go of things, ideas and people that you are no longer in alignment with, allows that which you are in alignment with to flow into your life. Let go of living for obligations. Stop living for "what ifs". Plan for great prosperity and abundance! Quit pushing against. Quit fighting for your limitations. Trust your truth.

Stop trying to fix others. All this protesting and fighting against issues of global domination, injustices, conspiracies. Just let it go. Stop following it. You will be ok...more than ok. You will start to notice your own happiness and contentment. All these ideas went through my mind as I completed the 1500 mile motorcycle trip, in the cold wind, from Sedona to Olympia in Washington state. The last leg of the trip was an especially long endurance ride (11 hours). As I settled into Olympia, my initial thought was to create flyers, contact Unity churches and really "put myself out there". As it turned out, it all worked out perfectly. I met an enlightened woman who had planned on being in Sedona the day I met her. Her tripped was canceled and we found ourselves having an especially deep conversation and became instant friends. Helen setup everything at the Unity church in a town in Washington and it turned out magically.

As I left Washington, I became fully aware how everything was perfectly taken care of, without me having to figure anything out. Now, in my one-person tent planted in the ground at Smith Rock State Park in Oregon, the geese are cackling nearby, tiny raindrops tap on my tent and children talk nearby. It had been one of the more challenging motorcycle trips again. Rain for 100 miles, then hail and finally, at the pass on Mt. Hood, snow. Snow on helmet that I had to wipe off with my gloved hand. This California-native isn't used to this part of motorcycling. I was reminded, as I am now in this very moment, that the sun always comes out.

Sharangati ; total faith in God

OWN YOUR WORDS AND SPEAK THE POETRY OF LOVE

If you're having trouble finding words to express what you are feeling, take this as an excellent indication that you are communicating from a higher place. These moments are sometimes perfect opportunities for sacred silence. If you absolutely must shift this precious silence with words, speak only the poetry of love.

When you are awake and present, generous listening will precede selective speaking. When speaking, speak from your heart. Narrow your conversation down to your truth. What is here now? Is it true for You? Once you've narrowed this down, now only speak words of healing and love. Humans long for connection, so connect. Listen with your heart. See the other person as a gift. This is what happened back in Washington. I was given the chance to share from my heart. I wasn't nervous about what I was going to share. I didn't have any feelings of inadequacy or lack starting the "Delicious Dialog". My message was one of Love and not about me.

When we communicate, sometimes we may find ourselves in disagreement. If you are arguing, try to let go of your investment. Realize another's belief is their truth for them from their perspective, history and life experience. Sometimes, we create an argument because we know that we need a change in the conditions, are the person to make the change and don't want to do it. If you honestly look back at any conflict you've experienced, it probably drove you to do something which was out of your comfort zone. When you lost your job, it probably opened up a better opportunity. If someone told you something that offended you, you were moved to stand firmly in your convictions or to take a deep look at yourself and thereby cause your own evolution. Within most arguments, we can realize that we are really just upset with our self.

People usually have preferred ways of communicating. They are influenced by these ways of communicating and their relationships tend to blossom when their preferred way is used. Some people love to give and receive gifts. It means so much to them to receive little gifts from their partner and are always thinking of their loved ones by the gifts they think will be perfect for them. Physical Intimacy or touch is important to others and you'll find them walking hand-in-hand or driving with one hand on the wheel and the other on their partner's leg. Quality time speaks to others and they live in the moment with their beloved. Still others enjoy words of appreciation and love.

Most people appreciate clarity. While creating a website for a client, I felt something out of alignment. I couldn't put my finger on it. This person had been a client for over five years. He always makes me smile and laugh when we talk. He's full of fun energy. That's why it felt so weird for me to feel like something was off. It had something to do with setting boundaries. I called him and talked to him about it. He received it so well. We got clear about everything and even doubled the amount of work (and pay) that I would be getting. He was thrilled that I called and wanted to help in any way.

The words you speak are imperative to the joy you experience. If you always speak in a truthful way, using statements which reflect your loving affirmations which come directly from your heart, then this is the continued gifts you receive that you deserve. Imagine there is a little gnome who is recording everything you say and then fulfilling your life with what he has recorded. He will do his best to understand what you desire by what he interprets in the words you speak. If you are used to putting yourself down and complaining about life, then those beliefs will keep being presented to you within the world around you. If you are vague and unfocused, your life will give you "vague" and "unfocused". If you speak only of love and gratitude, life will present those as well. I use *Facebook* in this way. Some complain about the loss of privacy and the incredible stream of data being placed in front of us. I use it as a metaphor for creating my world. I "Like" this and "Hide" (remove) that. Then, as I get more clear on what I want to see, more of that is provided to me. I also started to "Unfriend" people that I no longer "resonate" with, meaning we just don't have life content in common. If I attract them back into my life, then we've got something that's pulling us in. There could be a better word than "Unfriend", but it does the trick. I trust people will do the same with me.

On the scientific level, all beings, planets and stars are made up of an energy field called a 'taroidial field'. This taroidial field, in the shape of a donut, is an electro-magnetic field, which, together with spin, causes gravity. This electro-magnetic, gravitational field (EMGF) attracts matter. Whatever the EMGF is tuned to will attract to itself. This is exactly the same as our physical beings. This is all to say that what we put out (words, actions, thoughts), we will attract back to ourselves. It's just science. So, be aware of what you are thinking and saying to yourself and others and how you are saying it. Don't worry, we haven't yet evolved to instantaneous manifestation, but check this out:

EXERCISE: I'll present a word or a phrase and then give you something to replace it with.

"Need" into "Claim". Instead of "I need a partner", "I claim the best partner for me, one that honors who I am and speaks in my love language".

"Can't" into "Could or Can". The great thing about "could" is that something that you might think is definitely not possible, "could" gives it a chance. From there you move to 'can'.

Here's an easy one. "Try" into "Do". "I will try" has a couple things going on..."will" and "try". Can you feel the lack there? "Am doing" sounds and feels better, doesn't it?

"No" into "Yes". Ok, you are probably feeling

like maybe "Yes" isn't the appropriate answer for every situation. You're thinking of a life-threatening situation where you, or worse, your children are being attacked. "Yes" is the answer to everything. "Yes, an attack is happening. There's no hiding from it. It is happening." Now, you can make a decision to say "Yes" to survival by either not defending or defending. If it's your children, first know that they are also creators, as you are. I am not proposing that you sit and watch. Go and take you're your appropriate action. The scene was created for everyone, by everyone. There are no victims. That can be a tough pill to swallow. I know this can be a real button for some people, especially when you bring in the idea of child molestation and world hunger and suffering. You can never be a victim. Be brave here. There are no victims. You are in *victim consciousness* if you think *anyone* can be a victim. You can choose to justify the belief that you could, in fact, be victimized. But, how does this serve you? We are *dis*empowering ourselves when we choose this belief. We empower ourselves when we realize that we are always creating. Honor the creator in everyone, whatever that creation looks like.

Now repeat after me "I am not a victim, as

there can be no victims, ever. As my consciousness is ever rising, I now receive, accept and allow all forms of love, prosperity, gifts, miracles and fulfillment of my soul."

If mass shootings, bombings, wars and other crimes are still happening, then this means that they are a part of our world and the collective consciousness. If this is true, then what is a wayshower or lightworker to do? For me, the answer is to do things which bring me joy and fulfillment and one of those things is to wake people up. I don't normally have first-hand experience with these stories of darkness and are usually only fed to me if I take part in a controlled and manipulated news system, so this tells me it isn't part of my reality. Still, I can't help but continue to uncover and replace any thoughts or beliefs that perpetuate anger or fear.

This leads us to "They". There is no "They". There is only "I". Not the "I" as in the identity of you, but the big "I", the All-That-Is "I", the drop of water within and as the ocean. Before we get too deep in this ocean, let's try some more. "I could never" becomes "How exciting!". "How exciting it's going to be to accomplish this." "I forget" becomes "I am sure I will remember."

"There's nothing I can do" becomes "I am sure I'll find an answer." Here's one more. "Life is terrible!" becomes "I am sure there is something in this experience for me." Life and creation are based on contrast and preference. When we are faced with "Life is terrible!" we automatically have the opportunity to create a thought or desire of what we'd prefer to experience. Now, if we get stuck in the muck, even when there's no more muck in front of us, then that will continue to be our experience. "Yes, I'm in the muck. This other thing is what I'd prefer. Now, I'm no longer in the muck. I claim..." You get it?

YOU ARE WORTHY AND
YOU ARE LOVED

You are enough. You are doing things in order
to have an experience, not to become
enough. This is the story of your soul. You are
here having a physical experience, not to make
yourself enough. You are not a "spiritual
person" and do not have "spiritual"
experiences and are not on a "spiritual" path.
You, I, we are of spirit, souls who are having a
dream of a physical dimension.

How could you not be worthy? You and I are
both created from the stars. It's a fact. We are
comprised of energy. You are an aspect of
God. How could you not warrant forgiveness,
unconditional love, if those things weren't
already inherently given? Are you so special
and different than everyone else that you are
somehow not directly connected with God and
are not worthy of everything you ever desired?
We have the choice of asking for anything we
want. Instead of settling for something less than
our greatest wish, instead of seeing what we
can afford, dream it and envision and feel what
it would be like to have it and let the Universe

figure everything out. Be patient and feel it.

We are taught that as humans, we are somehow less able than non-physical beings (angels, saints, ascended masters). But, really it takes a lot to focus through dimensions into one dimension. It is known to be a difficult thing to do. But, we have done it and have courageously determined to help humanity evolve by taking this physical form. There are no mistakes in the universe or in creation. If you exist, you are perfection, you are magical, you are imperative to the completeness of creation. Your soul knows the truth of who it is. You cannot think how big you are, how amazing you are, how divine you are.

While visiting a Buddhist Meditation Center in Olympia, the Buddhist nun shared this, "When we say to someone 'You're so…[stupid, beautiful, ugly, smart]', we are not experiencing the truth of who or what they are. We are seeing our 'wrong' interpretation." I just experienced this. An older man, let's call him "Grumpy" seemed to not be able to smile and seemed to always share sarcasm and complaining as his main form of communication. But, when I experienced him loosen up and show me his beautiful, radiant smile, I was amazed! Before this, I did not know him and was not experiencing his soul. Remember this...someone having an opinion of you is them saying "I am having this dream of you...". While reading a letter from one of his critics, H.L. Mankin responded with "I'm sitting here in the smallest room of my house, with your letter of criticism before me. Soon, it will be behind me." I love that. Get it? "Smallest room of my house" – toilet.

There is a story in which a beautiful girl in the village was pregnant. Her angry parents demanded to know who was the father. At first resistant to confess, the anxious and embarrassed girl finally pointed to Hakuin, the Zen master whom everyone previously revered for living such a pure life. When the outraged parents confronted Hakuin with their daughter's accusation, he simply replied "Is that so?" When the child was born, the parents brought it to Hakuin, who now was viewed as an outcast by the whole village. They demanded that he take care of the child since it was his responsibility. "Is that so?" Hakuin said calmly, as he accepted the child. For many months he took very good care of the child, until the daughter could no longer withstand the lie she had told. She confessed that the real father was a young man in the village whom she had tried to protect. The parents immediately went to Hakuin, to see if he would return the baby. With profuse apologies they explained what had happened. "Is that so?" Hakuin said as he handed them the child.

Let any insults slip right by you by non-verbally saying "Is that so?" or "Really?" My friend likes to say (in his best East Indian accent) *"You can keep your gift"*. Also, when someone pays you a compliment, do the same…quietly, to yourself, say "Is that so?" You could add a sincere verbal "Thank you".

Stop living your life in relation to others and instead, create from where you are. Be comfortable in your own higher being-ness and you will no longer feel pulled down to other consciousness.

"When I was a young man, I wanted to change the world. I found it difficult to change the world, so I tried to change my nation. When I found I couldn't change the nation, I began to focus on my town. I couldn't change the town, so, as an older man, I tried to change my family. Now, as an old man, I realize that the only thing I can change is myself. And suddenly I realize that if, long ago, I had changed myself, I could have made an impact on my family. My

family could have made an impact on our town. The town's impact could have changed the nation, and I could indeed have changed the world." - Unknown

Before trying to change anyone or anything, there first needs to be Self Love. Self Love has to be the first step. Absolute love or healing needs to be proceeded by Self Love. Once you know self love, love everything absolutely. Does your healer, life coach, confidant, or guru know self love? Is the person you are getting guidance or direction from "clearer" than you?

EXERCISE: Stand in front of a mirror and say these words:
I SEE YOU, I FEEL YOU, I HEAR YOU, I LOVE YOU

EXERCISE: Say this, with sincerity and passion, at least 5 times. Now say: I FORGIVE YOU

EXERCISE: Finish these sentences:

   "As for my appearances, I think..."
   "I only feel loved when..."
   "I feel angry when..."
   "My biggest weakness is..."
   "When I feel hurt, I..."
   "My greatest talent is..."
   "My deepest fear is…"
   "My greatest desire is…"

Finding the answers to these questions can greatly assist us in uncovering our truths and removing obstacles to knowing ourselves.

FEAR AND DEATH

"Fear is the path to the dark side. Fear leads to anger. Anger leads to hate. Hate leads to suffering." – Yoda

What Yoda says has truth in it. Fear comes from worry for the future and not accepting <u>All That Is</u>. Anger is due to the feeling of loss of control (fear). If there was enough fear, the very thing that was feared may actually manifest. The objectified, intensified action is then anger, but this anger is usually towards Self, since Self is the cause. This all leads to suffering or the feeling that "this was done to me" and "What can I do?"

"Our anger or annoyance are more detrimental to us than the things themselves which anger or annoy us". ~ Marcus Aurelius (2000 years ago)

We have a choice of living our lives from love or from fear. Fear is something that is manufactured in our mind, concerning an event that has not happened. People who live in love, from their hearts, are happy and fulfilled; those who don't are usually not happy and are conflicted and controlling. In all of your thoughts, words and actions, ask yourself "Is this thought , word or action coming from love or fear?" If it is coming from fear, then it is not real. Are you concerned about what other people may think about you? Are you worried about what your family may discover about you? Open up! Let everyone know who you are! Your family doesn't know you, yet. Live life from love. Be brave. Absolutely refuse to waste one moment of your life marking time, hidden behind some fear of the unknown. Get out of the desert and into the sun. Ask yourself "What's left to lose?" Be brave and be courageous. We all want to be accepted in our "tribe", whether it's our family, workplace, bowling club or religion. This was a challenge for me. I held back my truth for fear of alienating myself. I realized that the tribe that I was a part of wasn't my real family. My tribe loved me, protected me, stood up for me…and it was time for me to move on. My real family materialized when I started to become fully my truest self.

Fear can really hold us back in so many ways. This morning, I realized that I had a problem with conjuring up a "worst-case scenario". I would imagine a beautiful vision, what that vision would feel like and I would find my brain drifting off into a vision of something going wrong. I know where this came from. When I was twelve years old, I was happily playing tag next door with neighbor kids. One of my friends ran over and told me that a police car was at my house. "What'd I do?" I thought. I had no idea what could be going on. I left and went home to find my relatives there and the police just leaving. I walked into the house and immediately saw some of my relatives. One of the younger relatives smiled and laughed and said "I heard your Dad died!" I was in shock and he was probably as well. I felt so blind-sided by that and through not wanting to have that feeling again, I would make sure I covered all bases. I would imagine the "worst-case scenario" and make sure that wouldn't surprise me.

As I started to "wake up" and learn more about self-mastery and accepting our emotions, I still didn't know what to do with these thoughts, as they continued to show up in my life. What has now worked for me is to fully and completely allow them. To let them come in! To embrace the feeling. To feel this fear and acknowledge it and not try to push it away or hide it. Trying to push the fears away never worked anyway. Here's what I did to process my fears:

EXERCISE:, Consider this statement: "I'm so (angry, surprised, happy) _____ at myself."

- Who is it that is angry/surprised/happy?

- Who is "myself"? Are there two of You?

- Which one of you experiences lack of love or anything?

- Which one are You?

- Who is having the experience?

EXERCISE: Focus on deep inhales and full, releasing exhales, then breathe in slowly. Think about the fear and scan your body for where you might be feeling discomfort. Money-related might be in the lower back. Decisions might be in the legs. Unsettling could be in the stomach. Sexual-related will be…yep, right there.

Allow it to be there and actually grow, if that's what it feels like. Just don't push it away or wish it wasn't there. It's there. Allow it to exist. Allow it to express itself and notice that you are still there, safe. Present yourself with what you are feeling: "I cannot help [my situation]" . Get to the feeling of this statement. Then, ask yourself

"Where did this come from? Is this true?" The fear has wanted to keep you safe. You are safe. "Thank you fear." Now, give it to your heart. Your heart is many times stronger than any fear. The fear can find comfort within your heart. Now, release the fear into the Earth, into the Universe, into Oneness. Imagine the act of clapping two chalkboard erasers together. Poof! Do you see how we've made the fear something different than you? Fear is not You, but a thought created from your ego. You are always safe. Breathe deeply now. As you breathe in, breathe in light and love. And as you breathe out, allow that light and love to go to and fill the space where the fear used to be. Even if this exercise is too foreign for you, just the fact that you are looking at it and directing light towards it, will make all the difference. Rinse and repeat.

At a higher, quantum-level, some would say that by imagining those fears and welcoming them (but, not becoming fixated on them), we are creating the experience in another dimension of reality and thereby won't need to experience it here in this dimension. Or not.

"Your power ends where your fear begins."
Pleadian Wisdom

If you've ever had a past-life experience, you might have a unique realization. It is one that tells you that your past life was considered the only life and yet here you are without a memory of suffering or waiting. Now, this life is the point of focus and will also fall away at the perfect point of completion. Death is merging back into Source Energy. When the body has received all it could handle or when its job is complete, it returns to Source. We tend to think of death as the person that we know is dying. But, only the body dies, not the animator.

Being in the body is like being in an amazing scuba suit. It beautifully helps you experience the underwater world. There is beauty and danger and your amazing scuba suit does the best that it can. Your movements are limited by the suit and you need to use a breathing apparatus to exist in this watery dimension. At some point, over the years, the suit will have fulfilled its usefulness. You can either replace it with another suit or take yourself out of this world and take off the suit. Death is removing the suit. Hold your breath for as long as you can, like you are underwater. Then, when you can't hold your breath any longer, grab the fullest inhale that you can. This gift of life is dying. This is our exit point back to Creator or

Source Energy.

Death is another name for change. Surrender
To death. Death takes every "thing" from you.
Your toys, your beliefs, your ego, your need for
food, your aches and pains, your suffering. Not
your love. Not You. It's all the same moment
when we die. It is no different than when our
bodies were living. Though, we will all
experience dying, we will never experience
death, because you cannot kill consciousness.

Why, do people, if they are afraid of dying, kill
their bodies with things that do damage to
them and cause their bodies to fail and come
closer to death? Others are fearful of death
and do the very best that they can to live
healthy lives. Still others are not fearful of death
(because they know they don't ever die), but
do not take care of their bodies and live in joy
of knowing they will always be. Finally, we can
take care of our sacred vehicles and not be
fearful of death. But, to be fearful of death and
not take care of our bodies seems to be an
insane way of living.

Apparently, our bodies weren't designed to die.
It's just the way we treat them. Luckily, our
bodies are constantly recreating themselves.
The cells in our body are cycling through death

and rebirth. Our brain and heart and skin and stomach...all being restored according the environment that exists. We create that environment in every second, in every breath. In the end, everyone dies from suicide. What do you feed your body? Everything is energy. What energy do you feed your body? Do you feed your body love, good thoughts, uplifting movies, inspiring news, physical touch, natural foods and laughter?

YOU ARE NOT OBLIGATED

I used to get irritated when at a restaurant and someone would order something custom-made not on the menu. As I made sure I gave my simple, easy-to-create food order, this customer asked for "lightly-scrambled eggs, with spinach, organic only, and some sautéed potatoes on the side...oh, and hot water with lemon". She would receive the order with a smile and eat her breakfast with joy and satisfaction. I learned that we can always ask for what we want. Whoever impressed upon us that we can't was as wrong as ice cream topped with pork rinds.

It's a crazy cycle of doing things for others through perceived obligation, not taking care of ourselves, having our kids learn from this behavior and then wonder what went wrong. Even if we are feeding the homeless out of a feeling of obligation, they will receive nothing of value and we will feel empty.

EXERCISE: Ask yourself the following: "Am I taking care of my body the way I'd like my loved ones to take of their body? Am I being nice to others, forgiving them, and giving them unconditional love as I wish my loved ones would? Am I living in the heart and choosing from a place of love as I would want for my loved ones? Do I show my loved ones how to live in my fullest expression, fulfillment and joy?"

Go to where you are celebrated and not to where you are tolerated. Choose to leave a room if the level of vibration or energy does not lift you up. It's your dream. You get to choose. Honor yourself enough to change your environment if it isn't currently serving you. This is not the same as going into a space and you are feeling uncomfortable. This may be caused by fear or the ego. This can be pushed through into something beautiful. Know the difference between fear-based and energy-based feelings. You cannot struggle to joy.

EXERCISE: Energy Chess

1. Enter a room, sit down anywhere, close your eyes and become calm. Feel the energy of the room. Ask yourself "How am I feeling when I'm in this room?"

2. Now open your eyes, and mess up everything in the room (try not to break anything).

3. Sit back down and close your eyes again. Do you feel different?

4. Put everything back in its place and
    check again. Check from a different part
    of the room. You can try moving
    individual objects around in the room.
    You can also move everything out of the
    room and start by placing one object at
    a time in the room.

Find out what lights you up? You are not
obligated to include within your reality any
pain, suffering, fear and worry. The time for
complaining about misuse, distrust, injustice,
war, hunger...is over (if there ever was a time for
it). It's a trap which perpetuates the illness of
humanity. If you choose to be involved in fixing
through force of will, I honor it. It just isn't my
reality. This is a time for new beginnings, for
creation of what we want and for what is
waiting for us, once we align with it.

Your life, like a dream, is an illusion. You have
faced the parts that you don't want long
enough. It is not virtuous to continue focusing
on "reality". It is fantastic to fantasize about
what you do want. This is creation. Focus on
what feels good and ignore what doesn't.

It is so tempting to become involved in the
news of the day. While staying at my Mom's

house, finishing One White Stone, there was more opportunity to watch the news. I haven't had a TV (except to plug in a DVD) in over 10 years. There's usually two or three "major" stories that get all the attention and are presented at every possible angle. It's easy to get wrapped up into it. I asked myself "Why does there seem to be such oppression in government and the activities we see in the world?" I discovered that it is because of the way humanity has evolved. We are so powerful and are divine beings who have had this truth hidden from us. We can sometimes see this truth in little pieces and start to realize our divine nature through the amazing lives of saints, spiritual teachers and humans with abilities that seem out of our own realm. But, like crabs in a pot, the other crabs will pull the potential escape artist back down into the pot. There has always been this aspect of humanity and stories of humanity breaking away from it.

MAKING LOVE WITH LIFE

"For me, continence [refraining from sexual intercourse] can be a way to Christ consciousness or to have direct experience with God", I heard a spiritual devotee say. I shared that I had been having these experiences of Christ consciousness and direct experience actually during sex. She said "Instead of expending your sexual energy on physical sex, you could be cultivating this sexual and creative energy and solely focus on devotion to God". This sounded a little self-righteous and I didn't agree with what felt like a sacrifice that we aren't meant to experience. Sexual energy is creation and to suppress it or not share this physical energy with another, well, it just doesn't feel right to me. God doesn't want and God doesn't need us to direct our physical, sexual energy to a thought of something separate than our beloved in front of us. As we see God in everyone, we experience God in all ways. How can God be something different than You or I? We were experiencing different truths.

How has your sacred union been with your partner? Have you been the one to initiate sexual intimacy? How does this happen? What do you say? If you spend the day together, what do you do? Do you set up the room as a "sacred lair of exquisite love"? Flirt with your partner, but do not tease or use sarcasm. Be attentive, but do not glom or overdo it. Keep clean hygiene. Through studying tantra, I learned how to create a ceremony and set the space before my partner enters the room. To take initiative. This could mean intoxicating incense, sensual music, sweet candles, bath with plumeria or rose petals leading to the bath tub. Invite your partner to follow the path. Bathe them...or whatever. I learned that our genitals are our sacred site and there are five different types for each gender. We can make agreements and set boundaries and then, communicate about what feels good and what doesn't. Learn to ask what your partner wants and have them show you. It's ok to ask.

I learned to be completely focused upon my partner and to also allow my partner access to my body, while I became in tune with the feelings in my body. You can train yourself to be so touch sensitive to activate energy or "kriyas" or even "kundalinis" in your body. During love-making, slow down. Be in the moment. Don't have an agenda. See what happens. You may miss what's happening in this moment. When you are seducing or caressing, be in that moment. Be in synchronicity with your partner. Synchronize your breathing. Look at each other. See each other.

While living within a spiritual community in Sedona, I met Gary Hendrickson, a feng shui consultant and man balanced in his feminine and masculine energies. He can swing a hammer and sing "a capella" in the style of Andrea Bocelli. During our spirited conversations, we both started to realize that what we were discussing was something that we were both very passionate about – Self Mastery and assisting men to realize their divine masculine and to balance their sacred energies. "Daniel, have you heard of the Quodoushka teachings?" I told him I hadn't but, I was very curious. Gary shared "Quodoushka is the merging of two energy fields to create a new energy, which is greater than the sum of its parts. These people offer amazing workshops on working with our sexual energies. These teachings have been known to greatly improve relationships and experience of our divine nature". The more we talked, the more we realized we were on the same path and we started to create what we called the

"Brotherhood of Self Mastery". Gary continued "Quodoushka teaches that even if you don't have a partner, there are ancient ways to "move energy" in your own chakras (energy centers) so you can have full body orgasms without touch. We'd sit in meditation or listening to music and experience these "kriyas" or activations of energy. You also can use "fire breath" which is a fast, rhythmic breath that generates sexual energy. The "fire breath" is similar to what I had been teaching in my "ecstatic breathing" workshops.

To practice the "fire breath" lay down on your back and put a pillow under your heart. Breathe deeply and start to focus on your diaphragm as the source of your breathing, instead of your chest. Breathe in through your nose and exhale out of your mouth. Do this deeply and to a fast pace, preferably in synch with evocative music and strong drum beats.

Every woman in my life, intimate or not, has been a blessing. There were one or two relationships in which I felt suppressed, feeling like I wasn't able to do what I wanted to do. At the time, it was very frustrating and even that was the greatest gift of love. If someone you are in contact with is challenging your inner power, it's because they or you (your higher self) are wanting you to flex your power...like a boxing trainer wanting the boxer to "Give me your best shot!" What more beautiful way for you to step into that. What being in your life could be more deserving of your love and appreciation for such a gift? When you appreciate someone, you are loving them. As in the movie *Avatar*, you are "seeing" them. You are connected to Source Energy, Creation, All That Is, Spirit, God.

Yes, there was also heartache, pain and suffering. But, these are not inevitable. Heartache is a normal reaction to the perceived loss of a loved one or the end of a relationship. The suffering comes in if we stay in the heartache. But, don't avoid the heartache. Feel it. Immerse yourself in it. This is living. Remember, everything is temporary. Every thing. You are in this feeling, physical reality and a large part of this experience is fully engaging yourself in it. To distance yourself from this reality is missing the point. Try to imagine yourself acting in a dramatic play. It's opening night. There is excitement and nervousness in the air. After your performance, you replay in your mind the acts and the acting. See your life from this perspective. You are an actor in this play called "Creation" and well, "All the world's a stage".

We are without form, except in our minds. Our minds create the Universe for this play.

Jump in! Embrace the sacred moments, the episodes of life. Wake everyone up with your life! There are the betrayals of life which continue to open us up to all that we are becoming or shut us down into sleep and beaten into submission. As the driving rain has drenched you to the core and spoiled your plans and you find yourself further away from where you wanted to be and can feel the creeping despair, can you raise your head to the sky, throw your arms out to your sides and yell "YES!"? When you're faced with a life-threatening situation or your own mistakes and failures and you somehow come out of it with your heart still beating, can you scream to the gods "That was incredible!"? When there is reason to dance your ass off, can you find the courage to celebrate and not caution yourself and instead fully express yourself and let your body fall into exquisite ecstasy? Can you be that person who starts the dance? Do you need a reason to dance? Will you use this life, and not another, to remember your true nature, your fullest expression, your divinity and your greatest love? If you'd rather sit on the bleachers, why the hell did you choose to be in the game? Tell me of this beautiful life! Tell me of the aching in your heart. Not for another, but for the unshakeable, unstoppable, unfathomable desire to live life within the flow of nature and the stream of spirit, to feel and give love so unconditionally and so freely to every divine soul and yourself, to deeply touch others with your open and delicious heart, to hear the voices as sacred sounds, to gaze in a stranger's eyes and see God. Humanity longs to hear you speak of the intense love you have for yourself, the long, sacred moments of silence that you share with you - the beloved. Show them. Your soul knows the truth of who you are.

Now is the only moment. Now is the only reality. In this life of never-ending contrast, you have created so many episodes that would crash you, but instead you have used them as perfect opportunities to say "I love me! This is what I choose. I will live and thrive!" And these episodes, some of them, were offered by those beings of light that you had promised to forgive. They were the angels that agreed to provide you with the illusions of betrayal, pain, agony and physical harm, so the lesson in forgiveness that you desired would be experienced. How could there be any greater love for you, dear one? Who could do this deed for you but an angel whose only desire is to serve you? The greater the deed, the greater potential for epic forgiveness. Can you even comprehend this kind of selfless, pure, boundless love?

Looking at it as a story, it takes on a new energy, doesn't it? Everyone has their story. We can all become attached to this story. Stop the story. With detachment, it's all so thrilling! Wonder what it would be like to go back and live those moments with this new awareness. You can. You can go back into those memories and experience it with more awareness, love and forgiveness. Yes, you can change the past. There is no past; only a memory held in your mind…which you hold the key to.

We are constantly experiencing and choosing to react or flow with our experiences. We interpret these experiences as "good" or "bad", but the episode is only presented to and by us. It is how we are responding in that moment that shapes us and any future experience that we attract or create. Someone dies. Someone is born. This we can call "contrast". Contrast is normal. If there were no contrast in life, we would not prefer. If we did not prefer, we would not create. If we did not create, we would not exist. There is a never-ending drive for us to create. Nothing, no healing, no transformation, no connection is too big. All that you do is done not by you, but by Oneness, All That Is, by God's grace your vessel is used to accomplish this.

When something tragic happens, we usually hear the phrase "everything happens for a reason" and is usually interpreted as there is something to watch for in the future ("just wait for it") related to this event happening now. We're supposed to keep looking for the reason that this event happened. It can drive us crazy wondering where the silver lining to the cloud is. Another phrase is "God works in mysterious ways". Ooo, spooky. Here's some more of my power. Thank you. God doesn't work in mysterious ways, only perfection. It can also be that this event happening now is the result of your creation, from your thoughts and actions. Nothing ever happens for "bad". Everything always happens for our highest good. With no such thing as the concept of *time*, our evolution and ascension is instantaneous. We can choose to see every problem or obstacle as the final test of your soul's evolution. Saying "Yes" to everything immerses yourself in all of the experiences of life. I thought that I was living life and seeing where it led me. But, in reality, I was already here and everything I had done in the past was perfection.

IT'S ALL ABOUT INTENTION

Jump into the ocean. Why are you swimming in the ocean? What does it do for you? Experience the feeling of water on your skin. Notice the increase of pressure upon your body. What is your intention? To cool yourself off? As you descend beneath the waves, can you think of anything but pure awareness and a deep, fulfilling connection with the flow of life-giving waters and movement of the ocean and its creatures? In everything you do, be present. Have fun with the question. It doesn't have to be so serious. It's not the doing or the action in our lives, but how we feel during that action.

My friend and I were having a chat one day. We were sitting in the Sedona dirt on the property where I lived. There was a sacred, spiral wheel made of stones, in front of us. My friend shared "I feel like there's something that I am going to be doing for humanity. Something profound. But, I'm just not sure what that is." We realized that if you want to do something for humanity, there is only one place to go. Your heart is the place. Pray not for others. There is not a problem out there. Pray to get yourself out of the way.

If you are being inspired, creating, intending from your heart with love and passion...and you are sitting in the dirt, you are doing more than millions of "volunteers" who are acting out of obligation or guilt. This is the secret to manifesting joy and abundance: Live from love. So, sit in the Earth, envision, create in your heart, open to all that is and know that this is all that is required for your place in the galaxies.

It's all about energy or intention. We are energy. It's not the object. It's the intention put into the object that gives the object power. If you are clear that there is no need to fix or change any situation and there is only to be in joy in what you are doing, then do it. Do it with your greatest passion! But, do not be attached to the outcome or how your gift is received. So, choose now to manifest a life greater than you could ever imagine. You don't need to be an activist or do anything. But, it's never too late to wake up. It's never too late to love and accept everything about yourself. Which life will you choose to be truly happy in? This one? You deserve happiness. No one gives this to you or takes it away. Demand your happiness from yourself!

What if we want to be a good parent to our children? Because my father passed when I was twelve and I felt he was such a loving father to me, I wanted to be sure to emulate that with my kids. But, what happened in my then unaware mind was this. I was sure to be the greatest Dad and then feel like I deserved something for myself because of it. I thought that I was being fully engaged. Actually, I wasn't. Instead of being the finest example of an awake human being filled with light, I also justified sacrifice for my kids, teaching them to sacrifice your livelihood, your joy and happiness. I was doing what I knew how to do, by osmosis from society. I know this sounds harsh or demented or crazy…do not focus on becoming a good parent. Your children are also divine beings, in a smaller body, and amazingly capable. Do not get caught up in directing them too closely into the illusion. Let them express themselves. They have had a shorter pause between this reality and All-That-Is. Honor this. By awakening to your truth and the fullness of who you really are, your role as a good parent will be the best. The best thing that you can do for your kids is to uncover yourself, to heal your traumas and understand your emotions and to realize who you really are. Teach them the "Art of Allowing". Let them know that well-being is waiting to flow directly to them, once they allow it. Practicing good thoughts and appreciation will attract more well-being. Imagine that! Imagine that kind of lesson for your children. Try to imagine that display of love. Your kids will learn to do the same thing.

I was remembering this thought about having intention, while I was riding my BMW motorcycle over the pass of Mt. Hood. I had three layers of clothes on. I even had boot covers to keep my feet warm. Still, at 2 degrees Celsius, it was cold. As I stopped to get gas, the snow started. It was then, as I wiped the new snow from the face shield of my helmet, that I remembered my intention…to serve humanity and have an adventure doing it. I had faith that I would have the most exciting adventure possible and still be safe. It's funny, I don't really have a fear of dying. Though, I don't like the idea of being injured. Maybe I'll even heal that thought, someday. Which brings us nicely to our next chapter…

WE ARE DIVINE BEINGS

Brace yourself my friend. Your body is an illusion. Ask any scientist that has studied quantum-physics and what our bodies are actually made up of and they should be able to tell you how our atoms are mostly empty space...a lot of empty space. Are you here? "Yes, by golly! I am here. I can see my body." Yes, I trust you are "here", as in present in this moment. Are you here? You are here and everywhere. Who says You are defined by the illusion of skin and physical boundary? Science has proven in many ways and methods that we are not solid beings with distinct borders.

Dr. Imoto (Author of *The Power Of Water*) has proven that we can change the properties of water by our thoughts. Our bodies consist mainly of water, energy and empty space. This empty space contains atoms which consist of electrons buzzing around at just below the speed of light. Scientists have found that these electrons are actually popping in and out of existence (*The Source Field Investigations* by David Wilcock). When the speed of these electrons was increased to above the speed of light, part of the object seemed to actually dematerialize. In what is known as a "Quantum Double-Slit Experiment" using a sort of "electron gun" that could shoot electrons towards a plate with two identical slits cut out of it, resulting in a pattern on a target in the background. Particles would act predictably and show a definite pattern on the target. On the quantum level (really small particles like electrons), physicists found that electrons sometimes behaves as a "wave-form" (which transfer energy) and sometimes as a particle (which have mass), depending upon if there was an "observer" during the experiment. Without an observer, the electrons would go through both slits, act like a wave, creating ripples ("interference pattern") and bounce off of itself, which would then create many lines on the target. That all was normal and expected. Now, here's the cool part. With an observer watching the experiment, the wave (of possibilities) would collapse the interference pattern and act like a particle. There was only one line for each slit, instead of many! Follow this out and it turns out that the universe is apparently a "mental" construction. This experiment is also known as the "Copenhagen" theory or interpretation and I have had first-hand experience of it. One late night, I had occasion to wake up from a deep sleep and needed to go to the bathroom. As a sat there on the toilet, the toilet paper was attached to the wall in front of me, at eye level. I remember looking at it and seeing a sort of fractal image of it. You might automatically think that my vision was out of focus, but it wasn't the same. The image that I saw was sharp, but vibrating as multiple images. The toilet paper holder hadn't solidified into a fixed position for a split second. Once it did, it "locked in". Another interpretation among quantum physicists is the "Many Worlds Interpretation (MWI)" and it postulates that the wave-form or possibility never collapses or "locks in", it just branches off into every possible outcome of every situation in physical reality. Still another is the DPI or "Daniel Posney Interpretation" (this is where I become famous) and it states that it's actually a combination of the two theories. The wave-form collapses and continues to be exist in every possible outcome of the scenario. Oprah, here I come!

Further experiments prove that at the quantum level, objects are "entangled", meaning once two or more objects are in close contact with each other and then later separated, they both behave as if they are still connected. Do you see where this is going? We are all of this. We are energetic beings created by our thoughts and beliefs. But wait! There's more.

Thoughts create beliefs. Emotions follow thoughts. Emotions, through energy, create the physical body. Your mind is giving you the illusion that your body is a solid mass of muscle, bones, organs and skin. Your body is created with your beliefs and your thoughts (in that order). When you search for the cause of an illness, stop looking externally (environment, other people, conditions...etc.), unless the foods you eat and drink do not reflect good choices for nourishment. Instead look inside for the cause (diet, emotions, past trauma, patterns...etc.). Probably 90% of illness and disease is caused by fear, anger, and guilt.

It's true that medicine can do amazing things to seem to cure what ails us and homeopathic medicine does wonders as well. As taught in the book "*A Course In Miracles*", medicine is magic. There is an object called a "pill" or some "medicine" or a "machine" that you will focus on and put your trust and faith into. These are all placebos. It may be proven that taking this concoction in order to stimulate that inadequacy will work to fix the problem. But, the problem is before the body's outward manifestation of it. This is not to say that we/you shouldn't take your medication. If the magic works and it makes you feel better, then by all means, use it. Only, find out what the cause is on the energetic level, so that it can truly be healed.

There have been many recorded and verified cases of humans living without food or water. This would seem to put into question the belief that we humans need food and water to live. It can no longer be considered a basic necessity. It is a desire. Now imagine that you were subsisting on prana/energy, sunlight and love. What then would you feed into your body? When will you be able to accept this idea? Until then, you know you can't do it before you even start, because you don't believe it. Fasting not only cleanses the body, but also exercises and disciplines your will to become strong within your understanding that you are the Spirit and not the body.

I healing technique that I have experienced fantastic results with is EFT (Emotional Freedom Technique) or "tapping". At one time, I had a very painful sciatic nerve, triggered by a long motorcycle ride. A friend told me about Lynn Mathews who practiced massage therapy, spiritual counseling and this technique (tapping). Before starting, Lynn told me to rate the amount of pain I was experiencing, on a scale of 0-10 (10 being the highest). I did. She next had me repeat some phrases while gently tapping on different key points of my upper body (mostly the head). It went something like this "Even though I am feeling this pain in my sciatic nerve, I deeply and completely love and accept myself." Then, while tapping (5-7 times) on the body points (lowest part of my pinky finger, eyebrow, side of eye, under eye, under nose, chin, collarbone, under arm and finally the top of my head) I would say something like "This sciatic pain that I'm feeling". I'd take a couple deep breaths and "check-in" with my body and again rate the amount pain to see if it had changed. In most cases, it had. But, sometimes, it wouldn't. So, we'd go back and do it again or we'd "talk" to the resistance. As unconventional as it may seem, it worked! This pain that we think we feel really is in our minds. Yes, we experience it as real pain, but can control it. We do control it when we created it.

EXERCISE: Energy Ball Exercise

1. Rub the palms of your hands together quickly (like you are warming up your hands).

2. Shake your hands out (like you are shaking water off of them).
3. Place your hands in front of you, palms facing each other (like you are holding a basketball).
4. Notice the resistance between your hands. Feel how there is a field of energy that fluctuates when your hands move closer and further apart.

THE BIG QUESTIONS

Who am I? What am I?

Give yourself a "permission slip" to explore this.
A permission slip is anything that reminds you
that you can challenge or question the
boundaries of your limitations.

Consciousness, Vibration, Light, Energy, Mass.
You see yourself as mass or form. But, we are
consciousness vibrating into light energy and
then into form. There are no objects - only
energetic representations or vibrations which
we (our brain) then materialize into static form.
The object or form never comes from
somewhere else. There is no other. It is only you.
But, you are never alone. You are always
surrounded by consciousness. What *is* reality but
what we perceive? And what is our perception,
if not our creation? Chew on that! I like to think
of myself in the following way.

A Bubble Within The Ocean

A bubble within the ocean,
created from water and filled with space.
Never separate and together always.
Ever recreating, expanding and ascending.

At the end of its journey, releasing.
Its physical form even had a name,
Its essence now returns from which it came.
I AM the bubble. I AM the ocean.

We can't estimate the size of the Universe. Every time we view another section, it expands. This is the same thing that happens when we explore ourselves. In exploring ourselves, we find that there are no mistakes in the Universe or in creation. If you exist, you are perfection, you are magical, you are imperative to the completeness of creation.

Spiritual guru, Sri Nisargadatta Maharaj, says *"Love says 'I am everything'. Wisdom says 'I am nothing'. Between the two, my life flows."*

In everything that we want to hold onto, we are nothing. In everything that we can't, we are everything.

Present a truth to yourself. Does it say something about who you are? If it does, then it is not a truth. It is a belief.

Sometimes, people want to know how I know that we are divine beings or the existence of God, Source Energy or Creator. Well, besides studying the recent scientific experiments concerning quantum physics that prove what we are, I go into the space behind my thoughts. What do I mean? Well, when I have a thought, that "I" is *having the thought*. Not the little "I" as in my identity, which comes after my thought, but the big "I" that initiates the thought, my breath, my heartbeat, inspiration and activates my body and mind. If I keep asking "Where did this thought come from?" I always come to an initiator not bound by this body and that's me! If that is me, then I am boundless, ever-expanding, ever-experiencing, complete, whole, safe, without form, with form and I can never ever die or be born. So, then what does this mean? You know it already. You are God. If you think this is some sort of blasphemy, then you misunderstand the nature of God. You have lowered the truth of God. If you have rules about what God is and what God wants, you separate yourself from the fullness of your being.

EXERCISE: On a piece of paper, write "I am..." and without judgment, write what comes to mind (i.e. "happy", " a teacher", "poor", "wealthy"...etc.). This is not the time for positive affirmations, just more of a check-in. Later, in a few days or weeks or months, check-in again.

1. Out loud, say "I am"

2. Repeat "I AM" louder

3. Repeat I AM, again, fuller, with joy, to the Universe!

4. Know and speak this about yourself "I AM the silent awareness that is here even during non-presence, noise or speaking."

To call ourselves, father, mother, doctor, lawyer or president is limiting to who and what we really are. Our natural selves are infinite, but we are embodied beings in this third-dimensional planet. Yes, you are playing this role in this time and space reality. Just do not become lost in that as an identity. We use these bodies as vehicles of perception, through our conditioned minds, in order to experience this reality. They are reflections of our beliefs, but they are not Us. The body you exist within has a lens to measure light with. Who is it who sees? It is not the lens that sees. Who uses the brain to interpret images, sounds and smells? What is it that beats the heart, activates thoughts in the brain and animates the body and gives it life? Who do we think we are that we are a separate identity and not All That Is? We were given an identity at birth. But, we existed before that identity was given. From that moment on, we were guided, directed, persuaded and threatened to fit in.

We are that which animates and ignites us.

Like a paper bag, poked with holes and turned upside-down over a light bulb, it is all One Source seen through many perspectives. You are in concert with everything and nothing moves without your breath.

Sometimes, when you know the truth from the beginning, you cannot be fully engaged in the deception, so we choose to be fully immersed into this movie, this play, so the experience would appear real and we could trick ourselves into believing the opposite of what we are. This is how we experience ourselves; by simulating taking ourselves away from the Oneness. For some actors, the next trick is to continue within the play all the while knowing that it is the greatest illusion. From this new perspective, a new vitality, peace and grace can be realized.

Exercise #3: Create your movie.

- What role will you play?
- Will you be the hero?
- How immersed in your role will you be?
- What would be the theme of the movie?
- Would it be exciting? Thrilling? Uneventful? Peaceful?

Contemplate this. If you knew you couldn't be

stuck in the movie. That "time" would not pass. That you could not be hurt or destroyed (like playing a video game). That you could gain the essence of the experience, feel it, know it…what experience would you choose? Would you choose an experience more difficult than what you are currently experiencing? Would you be the hero? What if being the villain would cause humanity to join together as One collective to improve their condition? Who do you need me to be? If you need me to be the hero, messiah, prophet or savior, then I am that. Isn't this what others have said. Isn't this what Jesus was saying? "I AM that." Isn't this what God says in its non-judgmental, all-that-is, perfection? Is it the villain that you need me to be in this moment? That is who I am for you…whoever and whatever you need me to be.

When people say "Thy will be done" (meaning God's will) remember that God is living through you. Do not continue to create separation between you and God. There is no way for you to be separate from All That Is. This is divine service. We become the served. How do we live that way, with the whole "Thy will be done" thing? You don't allow your ego or your demand for safety to direct your life. This is exactly what I was looking to totally clear while I was on this 3000-mile journey of faith. Living purposefully and without ego. God living through me, within me, as me. God is all around you. Listen to it. Feel it. We're swimming in it. We're a fish swimming in the water, not realizing we're wet. We decided to take ourselves out of the water to experience the water. Even as I write this, I am feeling Oneness with everything in the room. At first, when I would assist someone through some realization or different perspective. I felt like I had really served. Later, I realized that in serving, they were giving me the opportunity to serve and so receive. We are not serving someone outside of ourselves, because we are that. You are the person you serve. As I serve, I receive. They were giving me a reason to pull something out of consciousness to tell myself. I know it sounds weird, but it's almost as if "they" didn't really have a problem. I could almost visualize them walking away with a secret smile and deep satisfaction of causing an effect; the effect of me reaching into Oneness and grabbing truth.

Why am I here?

A guru was asked "Why is it that dogs will suffer bugs in their eyes when they stick their heads out of a window of a moving car?" "You have asked the most profound question", said the guru. "The reason why the dog will go through the bugs in the eyes is because it realizes the contrast, between having the bugs in the eyes and the exhilaration of the ride, is worth it." The guru continued "...and that is the same reason why you came into this existence. You knew that the contrast between the suffering that you would have to endure and the exhilaration of this ride would be worth it."

My friend Amanda says "Each one of us is a genius. Each one of us came here to express that genius, which is really God expressing itself through the being we call '*I*.' Ask the question 'Why am I here? Why am I here?! Remind me! I forget, what with all the stuff and everything.' Listen for the answer and don't edit it when it comes, because it'll be big, and possibly weird, and probably scary. But if you accept it, you'll feel a power rising in you and a joy that will knock your socks off. So quit hiding out, stop being 'nice,' share your love, lose control! Quit playing it cool! Let your Genius come through you." Right on Amanda!

Ok, so really. Why are we here? Have you ever saved a life? Created a life? Have you ever loved and felt love? Have you ever touched someone deeply or uplifted someone's day? It may seem like you just go through your life and it doesn't seem like you're really connecting with other people in a deep way. You have. You have more than you could ever understand. If you could only understand how you have unknowingly changed someone's life and how that moment then changed another's life and another and another. Just this could be enough reason for some. A flap of a butterfly's wings changes the world. Ask yourself this question "Why am I here?". What do you want to be here for? At the highest level, we are to experience God or All-That-Is, ourselves. We do this by causing the illusion of separating ourselves from singularity or Oneness.

We can be here "on Earth" to grow, love, evolve, express, explore, engage...etc. There are those that have taken physical form so that we can fully express, grow, love, evolve...etc. with ultimate selflessness. They are the amazing souls that have volunteered with unconditional love to help us experience these things. What about the people that live in a way that doesn't agree with you. On the deepest level, if there are people who, from your perspective, you are not in alignment with, then they may be here so that you can express to Source Energy what it is that you do want.

Your life may be transforming into a beautiful way of living. You can feel and see it. People comment to you and others how they feel around you. You attract radiant and awakened people. Then, the next day, there is someone who expresses such hate and anger towards you. What gives?

Sometimes we serve as the "hero" and sometimes as the "villain". Your loved ones may need you to be the villain. To Jesus, it did not matter which role he was playing. He fulfilled whatever was desired. You may be loved and adored one day and hated and despised the next. Don Miguel Ruiz of the Toltecs wisdom teaches in his book *The Four Agreements* in one of the agreements *"Don't take anything personally"*.

> *"What counts in life is not the mere fact that we have lived. It is what difference we have made to the lives of others that will determine the significance of the life we lead."*
> Nelson Mandela

Remembering your truth is important, because you have been programmed. You were programmed and domesticated to actively participate in the society and collective consciousness that you were in. We are all trying to succeed, make money, eat and live in a system that is and has been broken and was never meant to benefit humanity as a sustainable system. But, just because that was the program, does not mean that you have to accept it. Most everything that has been created was created by someone else and may not be the way you would have created it. If it was created, formed, and named by someone else you don't need to own it as yours.

Though, what is true for you is your beliefs which create your outer world. So, your outer world is a direct reflection of your inner world. Someone once said "We do not see the world as it is; we see it as we are". This outer world is this play that you are in. It's the drama that you experience. If you are unorganized within, your environment will be unorganized. If you believe people are out to steal from you, then you will be stolen from.

Present a truth to yourself. If your truth brings happiness, stay in your truth. Does it say something about who you are? If it does, then it is not a truth. It is a belief. Every person's truth *is* true for them and their reality and their perception. Question everything. Question all of your beliefs. Should I really _____? Can any of my beliefs be absolute truth? What is absolute truth? Is it? Really? Is there any thought that can be an absolute truth?

AFFIRMATION: "I now release all opinions, judgments and outside programming. I now only accept my own inner truth, which is validated from my heart. I know that every question I now ask, I know the answer to. I realize my physical as an illusion and a dream."

THEN THERE ARE UNIVERSAL TRUTHS...

The first Universal Truth: *You are the creator of your reality*. Your thoughts create your beliefs, which then are brought in front of you as your reality.

The second Universal Truth: *Your life is a mirror*. What is in front of you is a reflection of your thoughts and beliefs. If you have hidden aspects of yourself, which still can be embraced, these will be presented to you, by you. You attract like vibration and frequencies.

The third Universal Truth: *Everything is connected*. As the butterfly flaps its wings, weather patterns are changed on the planet. There are no set rules about what can and cannot be affected. We are all entangled.

The fourth Universal Truth: *You are already in your spiritual home.* There is nowhere to go. Your spiritual home is your soul. You cannot ever leave this place. Wherever you go, there you are.

The fifth Universal Truth: *You will live forever.* Before you were born into the body you carry, you were the I AM presence. You will continue to be after your body dissolves back into the Earth and the cosmos. Most of us have all felt that moment of enlightenment It's just that for most of us, the majority of input we receive tends to take us out of that state of being.

So. Who am I? What am I? Why am I here? How should I treat this "bad" person? How do I figure out where to go and what to do? What is God? Is there a heaven and a hell? What about people who suffering in other countries? What about terrorists and bullies and corruption?

There is only one answer, always and ever...Love.

LIVING IN THE HEART AS A CREATOR

What does it mean to "Live in the heart"? It's spreading pure love to all beings, because the love that you know, overflows from you like a levee breaking under the strain. Seeing the good/God in everyone. It's realizing that your heart is your power, your wisdom and your center. It's keeping that center through discernment of different energy fields around you. It's feeling your way (versus thinking your way) through life and living in the natural flow of life. Living in the heart is accepting and loving yourself unconditionally and fully, then accepting and loving others unconditionally and fully.

The Hopi say it's being a real "Human Being". It's nurturing yourself and protecting all forms of life, when possible. Living in the heart is knowing that a virtue can come through experiencing the lack of it. It's having compassion or empathy for all suffering, including your own. It's living life for your happiness, without obligation or sacrifice. It's also knowing the worst experience can bring about the best experience.

ONE WHITE STONE

It's not taking anything personally and being able to let go of anything that doesn't serve your highest good. Living in the heart is not allowing fear to be the cause of any decision that you make. Listening more than speaking. It's releasing all of the masks, the coverings, the beliefs, the judgments, the fears. Realizing those lies. Finally, living in the heart is understanding and knowing the truth of who you are and falling in love with that. You and I are creators. You are reflected everywhere, within everyone and everything. Your mind is everywhere and everything is in your mind.

We watch the news or read the paper and let others set the tone of our day. This trap that we can fall into. Fixing things. Protesting and fighting against. Sharing issues of global domination, injustices and conspiracies. I'm all for uncovering conspiracies. This is all a part of being awake. Set your own tone! Just let it go. Make the decision to filter out, to refuse to accept information that doesn't lift you up, to not investigate further anything that doesn't raise your vibration and ignite your soul. Instead, look for and filter in examples of love, coded messages from Spirit and connection with the Divine.

We have a choice of spreading love or fear. I

notice that the people who spread only love are totally happy. The others are not and are conflicted. There is no extra credit for being patriotic, for being a peace activist or fighting "for your country". You can follow all of this news and it's all good for you, but you could just stop and be ok...more than ok. There would come a point where you wouldn't miss it and would notice your own happiness inside. It's thought that if you aren't the concerned citizen or a faithful patriot you aren't a good person or you don't care. It's all crap...all separation. You could have been born in Iran or Somalia or Libya and have completely different viewpoints. Behind all of this, we're all the same. The next time you feel like fixing the government or the amount of violence going on...look inside deeply. Is there violence and hate there? If you have accepted a certain amount of violence in the form of entertainment, do not look to have violence eradicated in the outer world. This is another piece that New Earth Project is currently shifting; creating or recreating sports with joy. Playing sports that are more balanced and love-centered, without ego-driven agendas.

Living in your heart as a creator also means being the master of your body and one of the hidden and seldom understood parts of our body is our pineal gland. Your pineal gland is known as the "Seat of the Soul" or "Third Eye" and is considered to be associated with the activation and cultivation of intuition, psychic abilities, higher consciousness and the natural production of dimethyltriptamine or DMT. DMT is the molecule known to produce mind-expanding, psychotropic experiences. This amazing gland is actually in the shape of an acorn and this shape can be seen throughout history within paintings, sculptures, buildings and religious artifacts, attesting to its significance. It gets activated when women are in childbirth, when we die and when we dream (to name a few). Though our pineal gland can become calcified or clouded from the foods we eat and the fluoridated water we drink, you can decalcify and repair your pineal gland by not drinking fluoridated water or using fluoride toothpaste.

Ok, here's the part of the book that I've been apprehensive in writing down when I received it. It's almost more unsettling for some people than "There are no victims". I knew it was going to upset some people. But, hey. What the heck? Commence the boat-rocking! Even though I have enjoyed the taste of flavored chicken, stuffed filet mignon and barbeque, it's never done anything for my body. I get all the protein my body needs from broccoli or nuts, beans, or any number of other healthy alternatives. In fact, broccoli has almost twice the amount of protein as red meat, calorie for calorie. The taste benefit I sacrifice doesn't outweigh the clarity that my body now feels. But what about the people who say that their blood type requires them to eat meat…something to do with the blood type being a "hunter-gatherer" blood type and their bodies getting enough protein?

Allow me to relate a story. A guru gave a chicken to each of two men and told them "Go and take your chicken where no one can see and kill the chicken". One of the men went behind a fence and killed the chicken. The other went behind a building, then another and was seen wandering about. This second man finally returned, after several days, to the guru. The guru asked "What happened? You didn't kill the chicken". The man replied "Everywhere I go the chicken still sees". We are always connected with everything and, on some level, the conscious animal that is killed and prepared for our consumption.

Rarely, does one know the animal, how it was raised and in what conditions. Also, rarely do we kill the animal ourselves or know or want to know how the animal was killed. This is very important. Imagine the energy that is resident in the meat that you consume. If the requirement is protein and the question is "Where do I get my protein?" then understand that there are very few, if any, recorded medical cases of protein-deficiency. Malnutrition, yes. Starvation, yes. But, rarely a lack of protein as the cause of illness. We humans don't actually need the protein that we've been told that we need. The protein "requirements" have been given to us decades ago by a government-subsidized meat industry. I don't know but, for me, once I hear that an industry has been subsidized by a corrupt government to tell us we should eat more of what they're producing...well, it just doesn't feel right. Vegetables such as broccoli and spinach and foods such as beans and nuts give us more than enough protein.

If it is "gnawing" that you believe you need, then gnaw on something that's actually healthy for your body. What is it exactly that eating an animal does for someone? Our belief that we will suffer if we don't eat meat is exactly that...a belief, not a truth. A belief that someone is a blood type that is associated with "hunter-gatherers" is a belief and not a truth. How is this working for you and your health? Get up off your knees and take back your power. Quit fighting for your limitations. Because everything is not black and white, there are people who will eat meat and this is still very important to them. I fully realize that I live in a world where people still eat meat. But, I have faith that, at some point in our evolution, we will discard this idea and embrace every being as having consciousness and worthy of life. Am I saying that we cannot have ultimate health while eating meat? Yes, this is what I'm saying. This goes beyond the physical and into the energetic. We will always have an inner-knowing that just doesn't feel in alignment. The energy that is *normally* associated with hunting, capturing, killing, slaughtering and eating another being doesn't lead to a spirit-led existence. There are some indigenous people that lead a life close to nature and as brothers and sisters to the animal nation. Their killing is a sacred practice and is strictly for their survival. Am I also saying that self-realization, or higher realms of consciousness, can't be attained while eating meat? Good question. Though indigenous people may eat meat in a sacred and honoring way, realization is not an automatic result of honoring the animal and preparing the animal with blessings, then eating the flesh in gratitude. The answer is actually in the question. *Do not try to win a race with a penny in your pocket.*

Here are some additional things that will raise your body's vibration (make you healthier). Use organic coconut oil in your meals, cooking, as a massage oil, lubricant, detoxifier, mouth optimizer (check out "oil-pulling"). Drink alkaline water with lemon. Try sun-gazing at sunrise and sunset for vitamin D. This is where you don't look directly at the sun, but towards the sun and during times when the sun's rays are weakest. Increase your intake of iodine (seaweed). Iodine helps against the effects of radiation. Laugh. If you can't find something to laugh about, find something to cry about. Crying is a healing release. Practice proper nutrition. Fast once a week. Learn to flow with life. Love yourself. Ask for help. Follow your heart. Practice yoga. Yoga works to "wring out" your body of stuck energies and emotions and allows for more clear connection to Source. One of my most profound physical experiences of feeling the divine within me happened during one of Eddie Ellner's classes at Yoga Soup, in Santa Barbara, California. I was affected by the beautiful music that had been played and I was really into the poses ("asanas") that Eddie was guiding the class in. At the end, while in "corpse" pose (lying down on my back), my body became electrified and I felt every cell alive and activated. I couldn't move for several minutes. Right there in class, I burst into tears of joy. It was great. Eddie took it all in stride and it was no big deal. My beloved was there with me and comforted me through it all.

Have fun and play with life. Reduce cell phone time and protect yourself with a headset or other EMF protection. Meditate. Use this ancient tool as a way to bring yourself back into the flow. If you have a difficult time going inside to do inner work, meditation is a great way to start. Visualize your life as a meditation, not separate from "sitting down to meditate". Remember to follow your inner promptings.

The spiritual guru of Krishna Das was once asked how one meditates. The guru, Neem Karoli Baba, answered "Meditate like Christ". Everyone was perplexed. So, people asked "How *did* he meditate?" It seemed Neem Karoli Baba started to speak and then became very still and silent. A tear came down his cheek. After a couple of minutes, with great emotion, he said "He lost himself in love."

EXERCISE:

1. Go to a space which is free from clutter, noise or other distractions.

2. Sit either in a straight-back chair or on the floor/ground, with your knees lower than your hips.

3. Choose a position that you know you can sit in for an extended period of time.

4. Softly close and relax your eyes.

5. Let your thoughts come in. Welcome them. You can put them in your virtual box for safe-keeping for later.

6. Point your now closed eyes upwards towards your brow.

7. Focus on the feeling of air coming in and out of your nostrils, the feeling of different parts of your body and the movement of your diaphragm as it moves the air in and out of your body.

8. See yourself from above your body. Enjoy the freedom of this new perspective.

9. Be in the moment. Visualize your own light.

Our bodies are a living example of harmonics and actually have a frequency. Certain harmonics can create structure. The generic term for this field of science is the study of modal phenomena, re-titled "Cymatics" by Hans Jenny, a Swiss medical doctor and a pioneer in this field. Typically the surface of a plate, diaphragm, or membrane is vibrated, and regions of maximum and minimum displacement are made visible in a thin coating of particles, paste, or liquid. Different patterns emerge in the excitatory medium depending on the geometry of the plate and the driving frequency. So, the higher frequency, the more complex and beautiful forms that are created!

Realize the power of your own creations. Let go of limiting beliefs. Let go of anything that does not serve your highest good and what it is that you are looking to manifest. Now, is there still anything at all that could be standing in the way of what you would choose to manifest? Is something not going your way (beliefs, job, money, relationship)? Ask yourself "Have I prepared the way for myself or have I made it a difficult path to follow?" Usually, on the subconscious/border of conscious-level, we know what we are doing to block whatever it is. In the past, I have tried to manifest "halfway" or in a lazy way. It just doesn't work. I have sabotaged myself or feared a wonderful life out of existence.

I had always wanted to live in a small cottage, on a large, rural property with lots of space. I could see it in my mind's eye. The problem I thought I had was that I didn't know how I was going to afford the multi-million dollar price tag that I was sure it had. What I didn't realize is that my brain is not activated enough to figure it out. It was already done. I just needed to stop trying to figure it out and let it come into my reality. So, at the perfect time, I found myself moving into a small cottage on a 4000-acre property, as part of a spiritual community. Get into the feeling of the thing to be manifested. Be specific about how you are claiming it. What is it specifically that you want to manifest? Do you want to own that car, or just be able to drive it? Do you need to buy the ranch or just have the pleasure of living on it? This is very important. See yourself within the manifest. Feel yourself in it. Say "Yes".

EXERCISE: Visualizing A Lemon

With your eyes closed, imagine looking at a

movie screen of someone eating a lemon. You smell the sweet citrus. You feel the texture of the cool lemon's skin and how firm it is in your hand. As the lemon is sliced, you see the fine mist of lemon juice bursting forth. Finally, you taste the exquisite, powerful flavor of the lemon. Now, you are visualizing yourself back at your table with the lemon in front of you. See, smell, taste and feel the lemon.

You have been made manifest. To manifest, exist in that moment in the un-manifested.

> "Each morning when I open my eyes I say to myself: I, not events, have the power to make me happy or unhappy today."
> — Groucho Marx

On the wall in the house where I lived, there was a sign which read "How does it get any better than this?" When you ask this question, this is not just positive thinking. It is creation happening. When you ask this question, the answer will be a manifestation of something even better.

YOU ARE DREAMING

Your dreams are a metaphor of your inner world. Lucid dreaming is waking up in the dream. Dreams can connect you with the energy that your subconscious is currently experiencing. Dreams can also allow you to have an experience in order to gain insight and clarity. They can be adventures to other realities and can also be messages in the form of metaphors. Dreams of snakes are about spiritual transmutation. Water can be related to cleansing. Trying to run and feeling like you can't get anywhere, can relate to feelings of inadequacies in your life.

I find dreams to be amazing ways to interpret my waking life. Just as soon as I relate the dream to someone, I instantly understand the meaning. I will choose words that express the meaning of the dream and so derive the hidden message. Check out the movie *Waking Life*. It'll give you some insight or new thought about the possibilities of what our lives might actually be.

You are always dreaming. Even now, you are dreaming. Much like your dream life, your waking life can also be interpreted in the same way. If the rear window of your car was shattered. This could be a sign that you should "*get a clearer view of your past*". I use the feeling of my dreams to figure out the possible message. I ask myself, "How did I feel in the dream?"

I now die to this day.
To fall asleep within my dream.
Only to awaken in another moment of now.

ECSTACY AND BLISS

How much ecstasy can I handle? I guess someone might call this a rhetorical question. But, for me, the answer is always "As much as I'm willing to allow in each moment". As I sit in this coffee shop, there is loud conversation and construction and dish washing. But, behind all of this, a song is playing that is expanding the boundaries of my ecstasy limits. Is it the song? Or when my beloved texted me about a bed quilt seen in a store? Or when my friend stopped into to say "Hello"? Or when I thought of you knowing you would read this story? Ecstasy is our natural state and I feel myself breathing into it. If you were to walk in the door, I am sure I would fall deeply into ecstatic bliss. My only reason to be recovered would be to see your face so that I could fall into it again...and again...and again..into an exquisite prison of love.

Watching my beloved dance in front of me. I fell into bliss watching her. When I watched her dance, I was realizing..."Here I go...I'm falling" just realizing what she was doing for me and what was being done. It reminded me of a painting I once saw. A young, beautiful, veil

134

dancer was dancing for a room full of Sultans. She could have been a slave and painted with an expression of agony. But instead, Lord Krishna (a Hindu deity) was the one pulling her veils, causing her to spin in her dance. She was in an ecstatic trance. Like the painting, This woman dancing for me was ascending into the divine feminine in front of my eyes. I was witnessing divine love. Such deep, eternal love was in her dance. She was dancing in love with her body and the dance and loving me at the same time. There seemed to be only one being in the room. I was thinking that I wasn't sure I could witness her dance in public, unless I just embraced what is and allowed others to experience me falling again into bliss.

A few days later, I rode my bicycle home, while listening to songs from the band *U2*. As I reached the driveway, I threw my bike down and fell to my knees where I stood...more weeping as the indescribable joy of bliss took me over. Though, to others it may look like sadness. It's actually both joy and sadness at the same time. Joy of this bliss happening now and sadness that it was hidden to me. But, then bliss again, realizing that it will never be hidden again and that this is where I start to live the rest of my life.

Later that same day, while watching the foreign film *As It Is In Heaven,* with friends, I was overcome again into deep, uncontrollable convulsions of weeping, spasms, joy, laughter, shaking. When my friends would speak, I fell in love with their voices and, of course, great love for them. Their unconditional love was helping me to recover, but also allowing me to embrace the experience. I couldn't look at them for several moments. I knew that I would fall back into ecstatic bliss.

Breathe...DEEPER.
Accept...EVERYTHING.
Love...MORE.

"Lord, take from me what I do.
Take from me what I need.
Take from me everything
that takes me from you.
Fill me with your love.
Liberate my Soul."

I challenge you to live in love. Go through your day and find ways to raise your vibration and experience more love. I challenge you to reject temptations to watch the negative news, to not listen to or be a part of conversations that stay in the muck. Only allow your attention to be gained by creations that lift you up. There are so many opportunities to listen to or watch things that are supposed to be important to you, that are presented as critical to your awareness of the state of the world. This is a lie. Even if there is not a "cabal" or an "elite" group of super-wealthy, super-powerful people wanting the masses to be "dumbed down" and existing in a constant state of fear and worry. Even if there wasn't an agenda to control and medicate human beings. You have a choice. You have a choice to snap out of it, to wake up from the dream and not accept what is presented to you. This is how the world changes and evolves and it has evolved. The media stream wants you to believe a theme that says that you are helpless. Once you start to disconnect from this stream (it's never too late), you will start seeing the world in a different light. This is not the same as putting on "rose-colored glasses". You will start to see the lies. You will smile and, with love, say "No" or like my friend, Jim, says (in his best Indian accent) "You may keep your gift". So, yes, the reality presented to you is the default movie that is showing. Change your inner world the movie will change. The state of the world is inside of you.

OUR DEEPEST LONGING

We all want and desire to be valued, to make a difference and evolve. There is a deep heart's desire to give all to be all, to be self-fulfilled and to be filled with grace. Some call this "The Hero's Journey".

We've longed to experience the joy of love for another. We've experienced triumphs and failures in this life and have overcome tremendous obstacles and persevered. Our actions have had a positive and powerful impact on others. We've longed to have experienced the release of forgiving another and have reached out and comforted another and been a hero to another and longed for the same forgiveness and comfort. We've laughed until our bellies ached and our cheeks hurt. We have stuck it out and persevered through the prophecies, fears and cataclysms. Over the years, there have always been fears to be concerned with. But, you either knowingly or unknowingly have faith that all will be well.

Hope does not comfort you like faith does. Faith can be like a shiny, new wrench that has 10 different uses and you can't wait to find a use for it. Faith is the "wild" card that you hold in your hand and begs to be pulled before the card game is over.

Continue to experience elements of realms beyond our current "3D" world. Stop living only in the 3D world. This is where the frustration is. The 3D world is not setup to support your consciousness, so don't look for support there. You don't feel supported because you are looking for support where there is none. You are exactly where your light is most needed. Stay in the light. You are here to speak to those who are ready to receive. There is no need to convince anyone of anything. The people who are closest to you may not see you. People like Jesus and Saint Francis must have realized the same thing. Some will think what they think. It may seem like you couldn't talk them off the Titanic and it's not your job. It's all an illusion. You are a saint. Just be you and the right people will show up.

THE INEVITABLE REALITY

We evolve. This is the inevitability of our nature. The inevitable reality is not us destroying our planet. The inevitable reality is us existing in an era of consciousness, there is no more war, within or without. We create peace within because in reality, there is no "out there", out there. We are stewards of the land and we honor our Mother Earth, Gaia. We honor, observe and allow. We create magic and beauty wherever we go. We create environments to thrive within. We look within to reduce our inner contradictions and hypocrisies in order to step back into our declared integrity. We honor and respect the masculine and feminine nature within ourselves. We listen to and respect our intuition and honor our emotions. We value our partnership in team atmosphere of co-creation with each other. As a natural state of being, knowing our true nature and our divine existence, our greatest longing is to remember and reconnect with our own divine being. We also accept and know that all beings are not separate from us, are in fact aspects of us and desire our full love, compassion and guidance. Yes, the inevitable

140

reality is that we are bodhisattvas-in-waiting and saints, if we choose. Step into this inevitable reality. All you need do is make the choice.

.

An empowered and awake friend of mine, Shara Summers, wrote *Ultimate Freedom Game,* in which she offers a unique and profound way of experiencing life, empowering and liberating yourself. One section asks you to rate your life in all areas: *Career, Finances, Significant Other, Personal/spiritual growth, Physical Living environment, Friends and Family, Health/wellness, Fun and Recreation and Time.*

I love the formulas and acronyms as well.
CA-R=UF which is:
Certainty x Appreciation - Resistance = Ultimate Freedom(UF).

Shara states *"Love, Appreciation and Certainty are who you truly are and already exists within each of us as our birthright. It is not about having to create or manufacture them, by simply letting go of resistance all that remains is love, appreciation and certainty, the Truth of who you are is realized."* YES!

Here's Shara's acronym for Ultimate Freedom:
G.I.F.T.

G] Getting Grounded and noticing what feelings come up when a wave hits you.

I]   "I am" declarations, the "Illusion" and "Infinite Being" or "Infinite Power".

F]   "Feel" and "Find". Feel the appreciation for the entire situation, story line or script in your 3D hologram illusion by finding the lesson or the gift.

T]   "Tell the Truth", "Take your infinite power back".

S]   The "S'" stands for "See the perfection of how all this Served you to be more loving, compassionate and understanding. The "S" also stands for your Sovereignty. In the Ultimate Freedom Game, you are the sovereign creator of your life experience.

We are in this experience. We could be having a dream. Our soul could have placed part of its omnipresent consciousness into form (this body) or we could be brain in a box hooked up to a "Life Experience #2,784,554,342" program. I don't really know, though I like the idea that I exist as everyone. I get to exist as an incredible guitarist on stage or fly down a mountain in my "wing suit" at 125 miles per hour or play the role of villain that causes humanity to wake up, rise up and empower themselves. I do know that everything here is caused by our belief, our imagination. It's entirely possible that anything you can imagine is inevitable to happen in this world, on this time-line or another. It's these beliefs and imaginations, if we hold onto them, that can cause us hardship and disappointment or prosperity and happiness.

As humans, we like to think that we can understand everything, label it and put it in a box. When we get really smart, we may realize that nothing can be understood, in the way that we think and the boundaries and limitations that we think exist, actually don't. How do we *know* that there aren't billions of versions of ourselves, all living in billions of other realities? Knowing how much my brain fills in the blanks and works off of known data…how do I *know* that what I'm seeing, I can believe as fact? *Seeing isn't believing*. Either way, however this experience is happening doesn't matter. I get to choose how to live this life and how to react to what happens. I will do my best to wake up in my sleeping dreams and become lucid and realize that I can fly. I'll do the same in my waking dream. Fly.

ONE WHITE STONE

The white stone waits patiently in the pocket of my jeans. It goes where I go and yet leads me forward like a carrot dangling in front of me. I recalled my friend Michael's request "You need to bring this to the waters of Mt. Shasta". I have ridden 1500 miles, by motorcycle, within view of snow-covered mountains and camped until my feet felt the pain of biting cold. Eleven hours in the saddle almost took the ultimate toll, one long and tiring day. I have stepped outside of the "normal" way of life and loved every second of it. The road up to Mt. Shasta is open and my white stone is home. After camping several nights 11 miles onto the mountain, I finally made my way to Bunny Flats to hike the 2 miles to Horse Camp. Along the way, I played my didgeridoo and flute for climbers continuing on to the 12,000ft peak of Mt. Shasta. The day was sunny and I hiked the trail filled with peace in the solitude. With snow still prevalent on the ground, the streams trickled down to the awaiting mouths of mountain locals. I no longer feel that deep, emotional longing that I once felt in the coffee shop that night and I know why. I am exactly where I need to be, doing exactly what my soul has longed for. With a short prayer and a kiss, I gently laid the stone into the creek from which it came. Later, when I looked at the pictures of the scene, I noticed beautiful sparkles had appeared in the water, looking like tiny angels of light.

Well, we've come to the end of our story. I have enjoyed our time together thoroughly and am grateful for your attention and presence. I'd like to also share a few prayers and phrases that I love. Our evolution is inevitable and as my friend *Astarius Miraculi* states "The Universe's expansion awaits your personal growth."

DIVINE GUIDANCE

"Father God within, I trust that your divine hand shall lead me in the way of my greatest good and that your will and infinite love shall see me through to the light of my awakening. I trust you now and always for my safety, for my being is secure with you and I know that you and I are One forever. So be it."

This next prayer is similar to the one my friend, Charles Jauquin (author of S.A.I.N.T.), says every day. I just gave it my own flavor. It works!

MORNING PRAYER

"Holy Spirit, please put in front of me the angels you choose for me to meet and the episodes I can embrace solely to serve you. Fill my heart with more exquisite light and expansive love. I honor you and ask for nothing but to be blessed with further insight and inspiration, in order to be of even greater service."

Saying this prayer causes me to accept everyone that is put in front of me as a divine gift and I know there is a connection that we are to have. When I meet new people, I sometimes ask "What can I do for you?"

Jacquin's book (*S.A.I.N.T.: How to Live More Fully in the Spirit*) speaks about everyone's ability to be a saint. Not a canonized saint with authorization from the Catholic church, but a living saint. I highly recommend his book. Here's something else that I always keep in front of me to remind me of what's his book shares:

- I completely SURRENDER to Holy Spirit's love.

- I totally ACCEPT the Creator's will.

- I willingly INVITE the Holy Spirit to comfort, teach and guide me.

146

- I am here NOW. Present. Aware and living in higher consciousness.

- I fully TRUST that all exists in Divine Love.

Remember the tapping exercise, "Even though I'm going through this...I fully and completely love and accept myself".

RELEASE PRAYER

"Consciously and subconsciously, I now choose within my breath, with every exhale...I let go and release all to God/Source and with every inhale, I completely and freely receive all the divine gifts that the Universe is offering me."

Wherever we go and whatever we do,
we'll go higher because of our love.

One last thought about life from comedian and philosopher, Bill Hicks:

"It's just a ride."

ABOUT THE AUTHOR

Daniel Posney was born as an identical twin with his brother, Ken, and older sister, Lisa. From a young age, Daniel knew he had a different perspective than some, but it wasn't until later in his life that his experience would transform.

Daniel's life has involved travel to over 20 different countries (including Tahiti, Africa, Europe, Australia and India), deployment on two U.S. Navy ships, triathlons (2 Half-Ironmans), daughters (Briana and Caley), granddaughter (Athena), black belts in Hapkido, training in Reiki and Munay Ki, living within a spiritual community on a 4000 acre ranch, riding over 100,000 by motorcycle and 1700 miles by bicycle (Pacific Coast).

In 2012, Daniel relocated to Sedona, Arizona (from California) where he continued to realize profound, inner transformation. Daniel currently lives in Sedona, Arizona and Kauai, Hawaii and travels the world connecting with others who are seeking the perspective that he offers and to be empowered.

Websites

DanielOfSedona.com – empower yourself and transform your life! Connect with Daniel through classes, FUNshops and personal sessions to release any limiting beliefs and begin to truly love every aspect of your life.

EcstaticBreath.com – lie down, engage in a fast, deep breath while listening to evocative music and didgeridoo, Native American flute and crystal bowl. Daniel holds a safe, loving space for your inner transformation, altered states and higher consciousness.

AscensionEarthNetwork.com – through inspirational messages, multimedia, tools, products, classes, personal sessions and training, we assist in awakening and empowering our personal and planetary ascension.